EYEWITNESS VISUAL DICTIONARIES

THE VISUAL DICTIONARY *of* ANCIENT CIVILIZATIONS

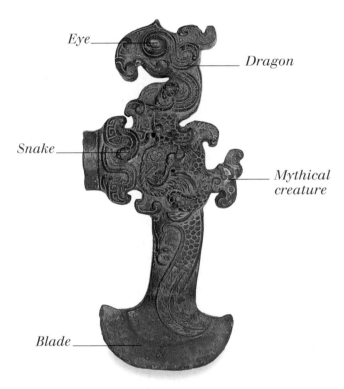

Eye

Dragon

Snake

Mythical creature

Blade

CHINESE RITUAL AXE

Worker mixing grain

Worker pulping grain

Beer jar

EGYPTIAN MODEL OF WORKERS MAKING BEER

Tufted owl

Pillar with flattened top

Eye protector

Studded decoration

ROMAN HORSE ARMOUR

Handle

Goddess

Bird

Splayed leg

CHINESE RITUAL VESSEL

MINOAN PENDANT

Moon

Red Sun

Gateway to heaven

Owner of the tomb

Dragon

Giant holding up the terrestrial world

MAYAN VESSEL DECORATION SHOWING THE BALL-GAME

Ball-game player

Glyph

CHINESE SILK BANNER

Black body paint

Protection for one foot

Rubber ball

EYEWITNESS VISUAL DICTIONARIES

THE VISUAL DICTIONARY *of* ANCIENT CIVILIZATIONS

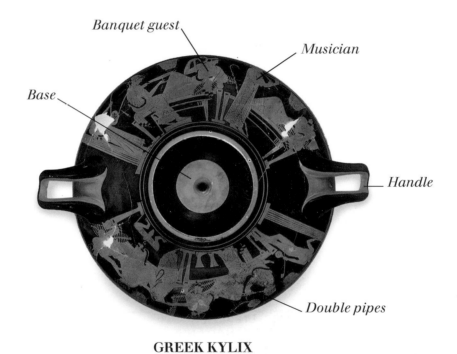

Banquet guest

Musician

Base

Handle

Double pipes

**GREEK KYLIX
(DRINKING CUP)**

Bird head-dress

*Ball-game
player*

Protection for one knee

DORLING KINDERSLEY
LONDON • NEW YORK • STUTTGART

A DORLING KINDERSLEY BOOK

ART EDITOR CLARE SHEDDEN
DESIGNER SUSAN KNIGHT

PROJECT EDITOR LOUISE TUCKER
EDITOR EMILY HILL
CONSULTANT EDITORS JAMES HARPUR, CHRIS SCARRE,
ANTHONY SHELTON, GREGORY IRVINE, T. RICHARD BLURTON

MANAGING ART EDITOR PHILIP GILDERDALE
MANAGING EDITOR RUTH MIDGLEY

ILLUSTRATIONS MALTINGS PARTNERSHIP

PRODUCTION HILARY STEPHENS

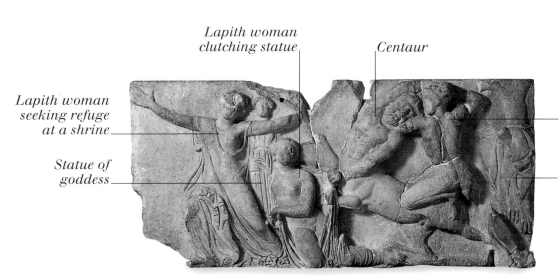

*Lapith woman
clutching statue*

Centaur

*Lapith woman
seeking refuge
at a shrine*

*Lapith youth
attacking centaur*

*Statue of
goddess*

*Panther skin hanging
on a tree, indicating
a sacred grove*

**FRIEZE SHOWING LAPITHS AND CENTAURS FIGHTING,
FROM THE TEMPLE AT BASSAE, GREECE**

FIRST PUBLISHED IN GREAT BRITAIN IN 1994
BY DORLING KINDERSLEY LIMITED,
9 HENRIETTA STREET, LONDON WC2E 8PS

A CIP CATALOGUE RECORD FOR THIS BOOK IS AVAILABLE FROM THE BRITISH LIBRARY

ISBN 0 7513 1056 5

REPRODUCED BY COLOURSCAN, SINGAPORE
PRINTED AND BOUND BY ARNOLDO MONDADORI, VERONA, ITALY

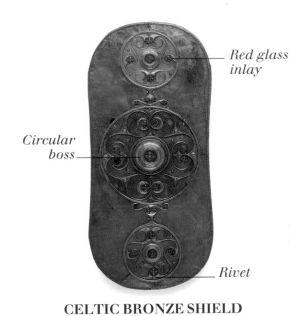

Red glass inlay

Circular boss

Rivet

CELTIC BRONZE SHIELD

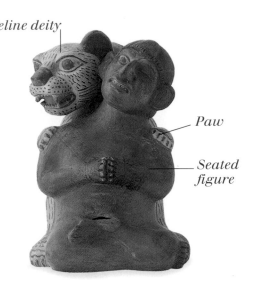

Feline deity

Paw

Seated figure

ANDEAN POT

Contents

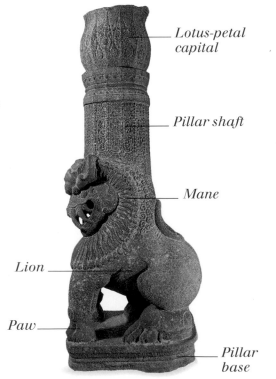

Antler head-dress

Decorated cloak

Ritual puncture

NORTH AMERICAN BOWL

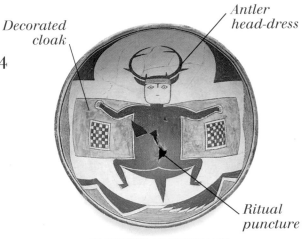

Arched doorway

Roof terrace

Window

EGYPTIAN MODEL OF A HOUSE

Topknot

Hair ornament

Silk robe

Leaf pattern

CHINESE TOMB FIGURES

Lotus-petal capital

Pillar shaft

Mane

Lion

Paw

Pillar base

INDIAN LION PILLAR

Mesopotamia: everyday life

MESOPOTAMIA, IN THE MIDDLE EAST, was the site of one of the earliest known civilizations. Between 4000 and 3000 BC, the Sumerians of southern Mesopotamia built the first cities in the world on the fertile plain between the rivers Tigris and Euphrates. Sumerian cities, such as Uruk and Ur, were enclosed by walls and had temples raised on top of ziggurats – huge, stepped pyramids with flat tops. The Sumerians were efficient farmers, using irrigation to water pastures and crops. Domesticated animals, such as goats and cows, were reared on the pastures and provided a constant supply of meat, milk, butter, and skins. The Sumerians also developed one of the earliest known forms of writing, which they used to keep records of livestock, food, and other goods. Scribes (professional writers) used a sharpened reed stylus to inscribe simple pictures, known as pictographs, on clay tablets. Gradually the pictographs became more abstract, eventually developing into a new form of script, known as cuneiform, which was written using styluses with wedge-shaped tips. Documents and letters written in cuneiform were "signed" with a cylinder seal – a small, engraved, cylinder-shaped stone – that was rolled across clay tablets to produce a continuous pattern.

CYLINDER SEAL

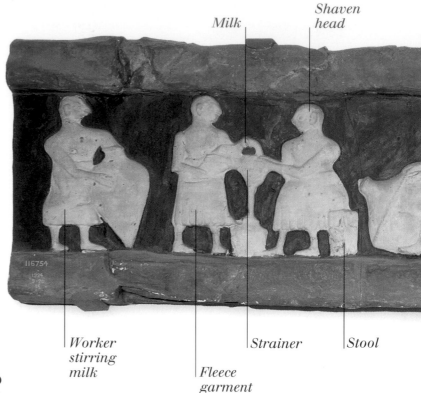

Milk

Shaven head

Worker stirring milk

Fleece garment

Strainer

Stool

CLAY TABLET WITH PICTOGRAPHIC RECORD OF DAILY RATIONS

Symbol for a commodity

Symbol for a commodity

Symbol for one unit

Symbol for day one

Symbol for day two

Symbol for day three

Part of symbol for day four

Symbol for day five

Symbol for a commodity

Symbol for 10 units

Symbol for a commodity

Symbol for a commodity

CLAY TABLETS WITH EARLY PICTOGRAPHS

Symbol for 10

Symbol for 10

Animal, possibly a sheep

Animal, possibly a goat

CAST OF FRIEZE FROM TEMPLE OF NINHURSAG, TELL 'UBAID

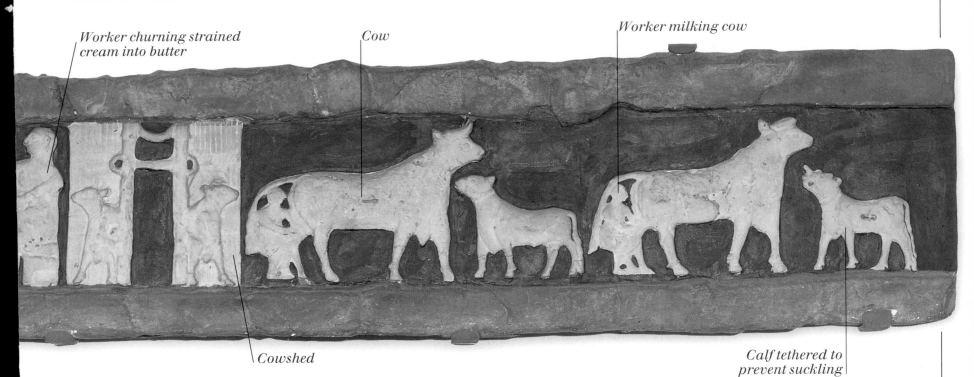

Worker churning strained cream into butter

Cow

Worker milking cow

Cowshed

Calf tethered to prevent suckling

COPPER FIGURINE WITH CUNEIFORM TEXT FROM TEMPLE OF INANNA, URUK

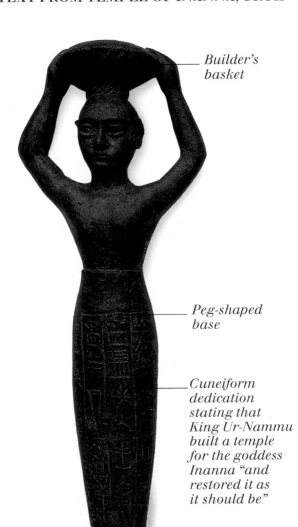

Builder's basket

Peg-shaped base

Cuneiform dedication stating that King Ur-Nammu built a temple for the goddess Inanna "and restored it as it should be"

CYLINDER SEALS WITH IMPRESSIONS

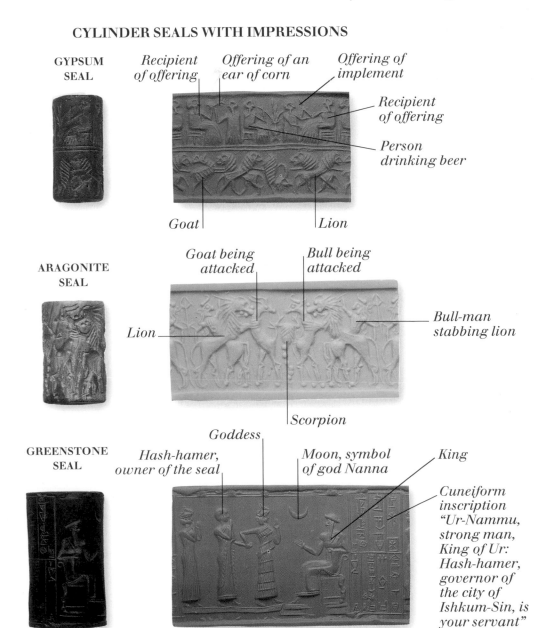

GYPSUM SEAL

Recipient of offering

Offering of an ear of corn

Offering of implement

Recipient of offering

Person drinking beer

Goat

Lion

ARAGONITE SEAL

Goat being attacked

Bull being attacked

Lion

Bull-man stabbing lion

Scorpion

GREENSTONE SEAL

Goddess

Hash-hamer, owner of the seal

Moon, symbol of god Nanna

King

Cuneiform inscription "Ur-Nammu, strong man, King of Ur: Hash-hamer, governor of the city of Ishkum-Sin, is your servant"

Mesopotamia: the graves at Ur

THE SUMERIAN CITY OF UR was one of the world's first cities. Within its walls were important graves, dating from around 2500 BC. Some contained spectacular treasures that reveal the skill and artistry of the Sumerians. There were functional items, such as chariots and rein rings, and decorative objects, such as two stands in the form of a goat behind a flowering shrub. The most elaborate graves were stone or mud brick chambers, some of which contained not only the body of the tomb owner, but also those of many attendants who were either sacrificed or committed ritual suicide. Many attendants went into the grave wearing fine jewellery and playing musical instruments. One of the most interesting objects, the so-called "Standard of Ur", is a decorated wooden box, which may have been part of a lyre. Its two largest sides are known as the War side, because it shows soldiers and war chariots, and the Peace side, which probably shows a celebratory banquet.

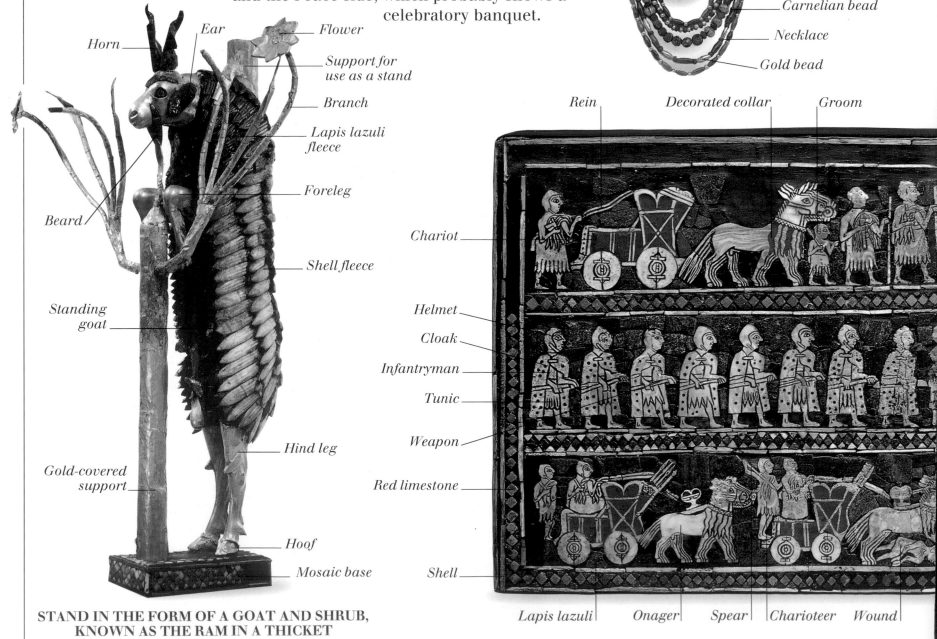

Gold rosette

Three-pronged head-dress

Gold leaf

Crescent-shaped earring

Lapis lazuli and gold collar

Lapis lazuli bead

Carnelian bead

Necklace

Gold bead

Horn

Ear

Flower

Support for use as a stand

Branch

Lapis lazuli fleece

Foreleg

Beard

Shell fleece

Standing goat

Gold-covered support

Hind leg

Hoof

Mosaic base

STAND IN THE FORM OF A GOAT AND SHRUB, KNOWN AS THE RAM IN A THICKET

Rein

Decorated collar

Groom

Chariot

Helmet

Cloak

Infantryman

Tunic

Weapon

Red limestone

Shell

Lapis lazuli

Onager

Spear

Charioteer

Wound

"STANDARD OF UR", PEACE SIDE

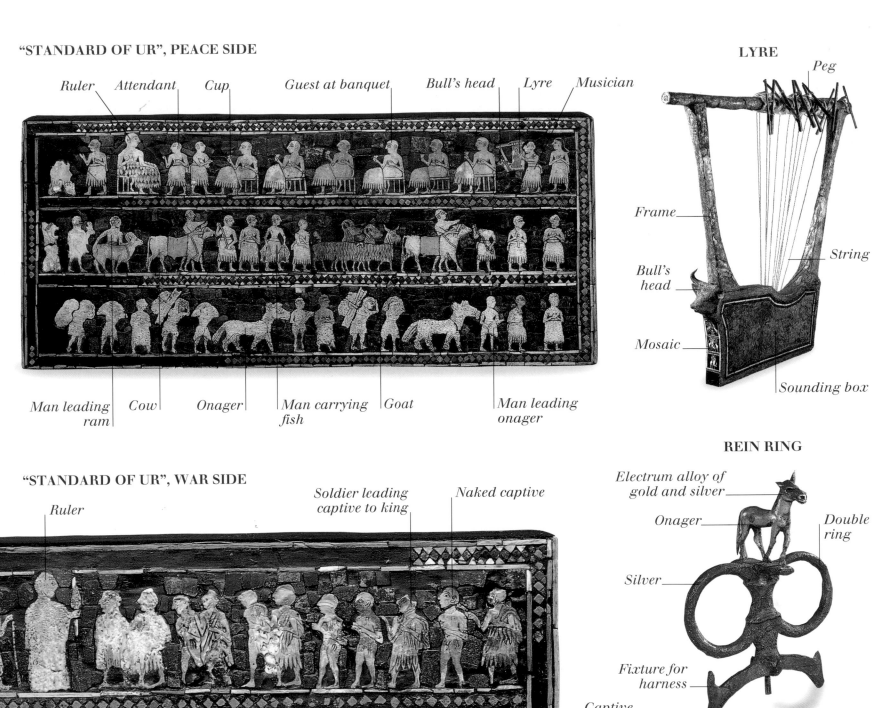

Ruler   Attendant   Cup   Guest at banquet   Bull's head   Lyre   Musician

Man leading ram   Cow   Onager   Man carrying fish   Goat   Man leading onager

LYRE

Peg

Frame

String

Bull's head

Mosaic

Sounding box

"STANDARD OF UR", WAR SIDE

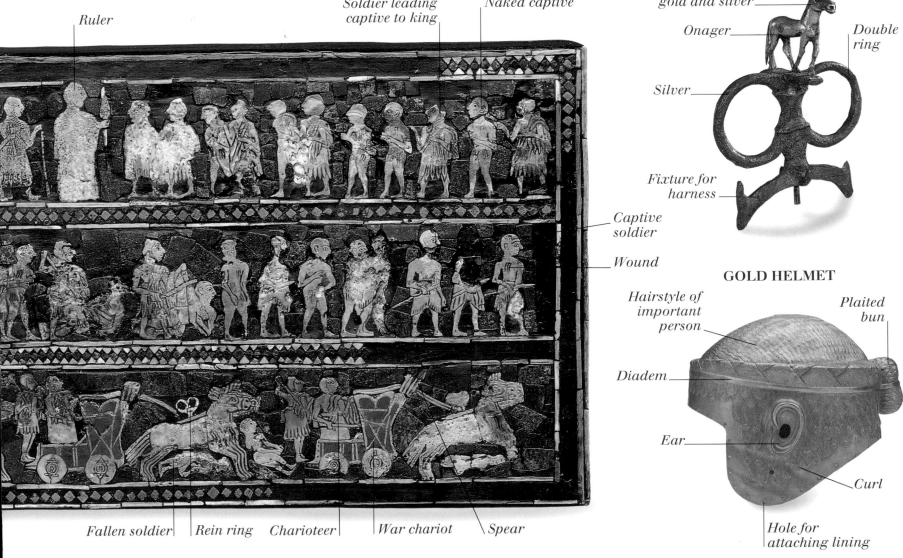

Ruler   Soldier leading captive to king   Naked captive

Captive soldier

Wound

Fallen soldier   Rein ring   Charioteer   War chariot   Spear

REIN RING

Electrum alloy of gold and silver

Onager

Double ring

Silver

Fixture for harness

GOLD HELMET

Hairstyle of important person

Plaited bun

Diadem

Ear

Curl

Hole for attaching lining

Egypt: pyramids and temples

THE FOUNDATIONS of Egyptian civilization were laid in about 3000 BC when Egypt was first unified under the control of a single king. The king, known as the pharaoh, controlled the vast resources of the Egyptian state and used these for ambitious building projects. The earlier Egyptian rulers built enormous pyramid tombs for themselves. Later kings concentrated their efforts on temples, the largest of which had hypostyle halls with painted columns and capitals in the form of a lotus flower, papyrus plant, or palm leaf. The first Egyptian pyramid was built at Saqqara as a stepped structure. The Meidum pyramid was originally built in seven steps around a central core, and the whole building was faced with limestone to form smooth sides. This pyramid was unstable, however, and the outer layers soon fell away. The Bent pyramid at Dahshur was built with a greater inward slope on its upper part for stability. The most impressive pyramids are those at Giza, which are smooth-sided or "true" pyramids.

SPHINX AND KING KHAFRE'S PYRAMID

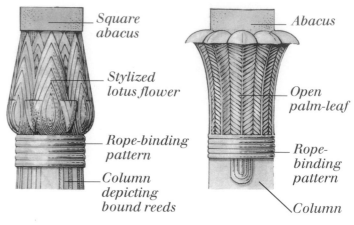

EGYPTIAN CAPITALS

- Square abacus
- Stylized lotus flower
- Rope-binding pattern
- Column depicting bound reeds

LOTUS-FLOWER CAPITAL

- Abacus
- Open palm-leaf
- Rope-binding pattern
- Column

PALM-LEAF CAPITAL

THE HYPOSTYLE HALL, TEMPLE OF AMON-RE, KARNAK

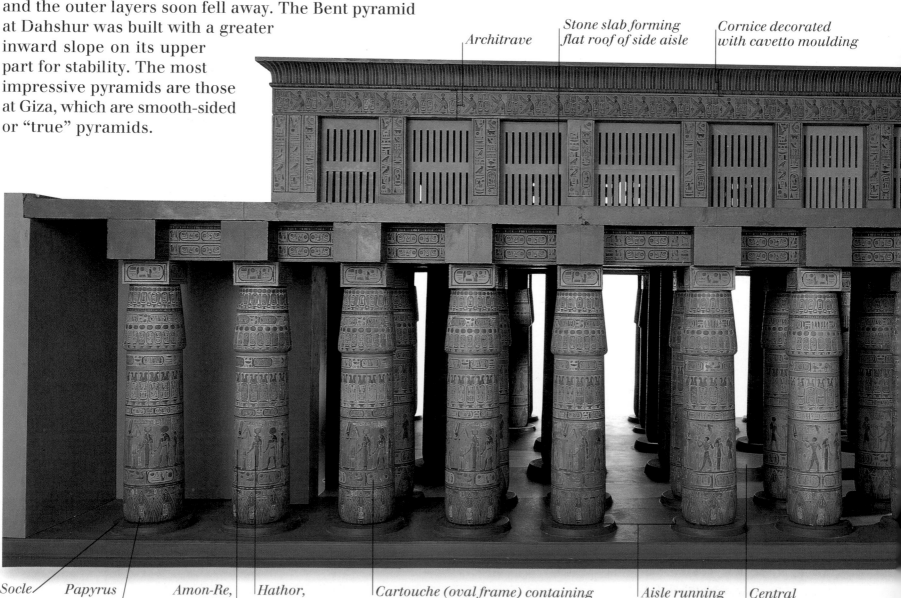

- Architrave
- Stone slab forming flat roof of side aisle
- Cornice decorated with cavetto moulding
- Socle
- Papyrus motif
- Amon-Re, principal god
- Hathor, a goddess
- Cartouche (oval frame) containing the titles of King Ramesses II
- Aisle running north-south
- Central nave

THE STEP PYRAMID AT SAQQARA

Entrance to pyramid

THE PYRAMID AT MEIDUM

Facing of fifth step

Remains of sixth step

Area of fourth step (now fallen away)

Area of third step (now fallen away)

Rubble covering first and second steps

THE PYRAMIDS AT DAHSHUR

Bent pyramid

Subsidiary pyramid

THE PYRAMIDS AT GIZA

King Khafre's pyramid

King Khufu's Great Pyramid

King Menkaure's pyramid

Pyramids for the three chief wives of King Menkaure

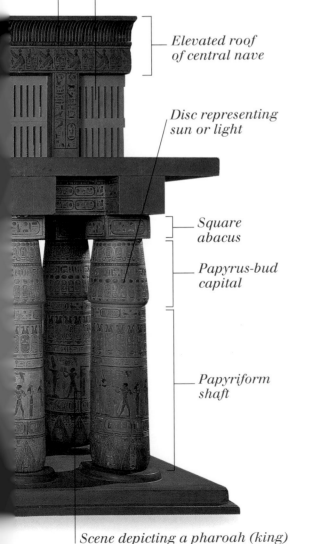

Bead moulding

Stone trellis window

Elevated roof of central nave

Disc representing sun or light

Square abacus

Papyrus-bud capital

Papyriform shaft

Scene depicting a pharoah (king) paying homage to the god Amon-Re

KING KHUFU'S PYRAMID COMPLEX AT GIZA

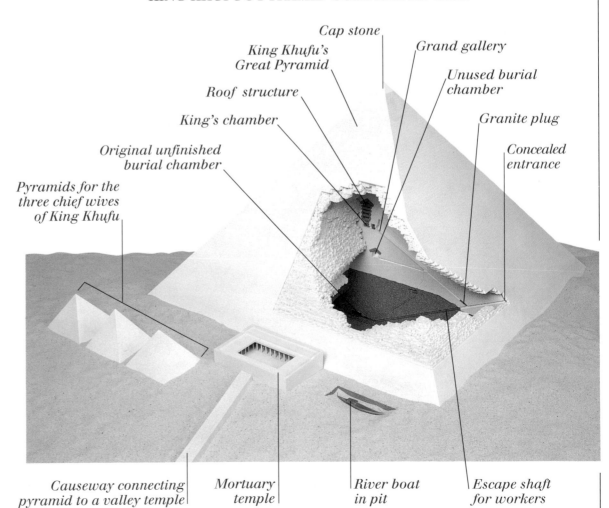

Cap stone

King Khufu's Great Pyramid

Grand gallery

Roof structure

Unused burial chamber

King's chamber

Granite plug

Original unfinished burial chamber

Concealed entrance

Pyramids for the three chief wives of King Khufu

Causeway connecting pyramid to a valley temple

Mortuary temple

River boat in pit

Escape shaft for workers

Egypt: everyday life

ANCIENT EGYPT was a bureaucratic and centralized state ruled by the pharaoh. He exacted taxes from his citizens to support the court as well as the religious and administrative systems. Careful records of produce and taxes were kept by professional writers known as scribes. All scribes and officials enjoyed a high status in Egyptian society. Other people with special skills, such as carpenters, jewellers, and sculptors, were valued as craftspeople, and some were employed to work directly for the state as royal artisans. Most of the population, however, were agricultural labourers or servants in the houses of the wealthy. Agricultural work included raising cattle on pasture lands and cultivating crops, such as barley and wheat, in the rich silt deposited by the annual flooding of the River Nile. As the floodwaters receded, labourers would have repaired the damage caused to bridges, roads, canals, and cultivation plots.

FAIENCE DRINKING CUP

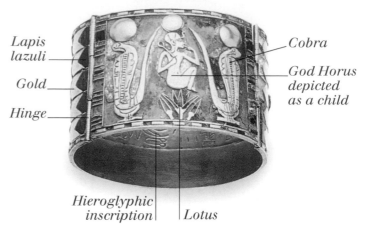

INLAID GOLD BRACELET

Lapis lazuli

Gold

Hinge

Cobra

God Horus depicted as a child

Hieroglyphic inscription

Lotus

GOLD RINGS

Scarab

Swivel

Sphinx

Ankh (symbol of life)

Lapis lazuli

Swivel

Glazed steatite (stone)

Gold

Gold

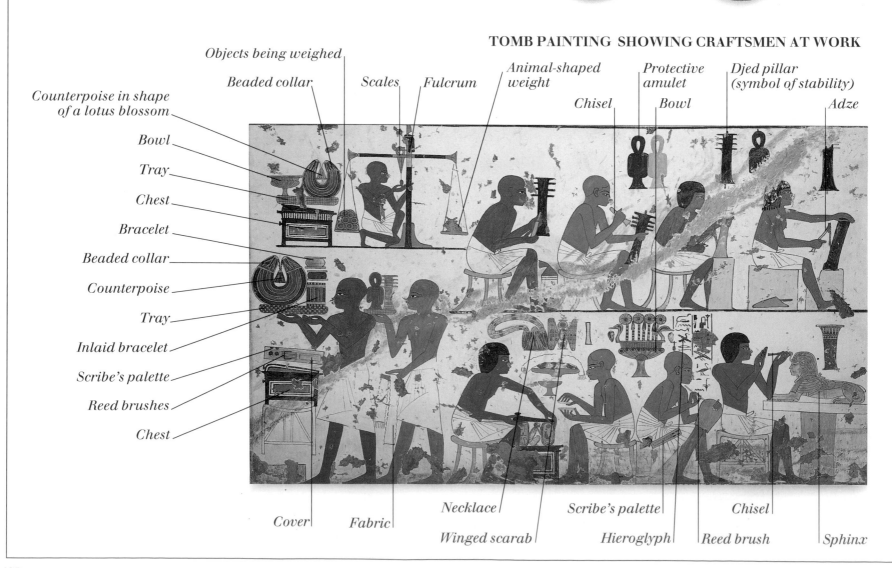

TOMB PAINTING SHOWING CRAFTSMEN AT WORK

Objects being weighed

Beaded collar

Scales

Fulcrum

Animal-shaped weight

Protective amulet

Djed pillar (symbol of stability)

Chisel

Bowl

Adze

Counterpoise in shape of a lotus blossom

Bowl

Tray

Chest

Bracelet

Beaded collar

Counterpoise

Tray

Inlaid bracelet

Scribe's palette

Reed brushes

Chest

Cover

Fabric

Necklace

Winged scarab

Scribe's palette

Hieroglyph

Chisel

Reed brush

Sphinx

WOODEN MODELS OF WORKERS

Bread and cakes

Basket

WORKER CARRYING A BASKET

Worker pulping grain

Worker mixing grain

Beer jar

Worker mixing grain

WORKERS MAKING BEER

Worker fanning fire

Worker kneading bread

Moulds filled with bread

Dough

WORKERS MAKING BREAD

Ox

Ploughman

Wooden plough

WORKER PLOUGHING

TOMB PAINTING SHOWING A HARVEST SCENE

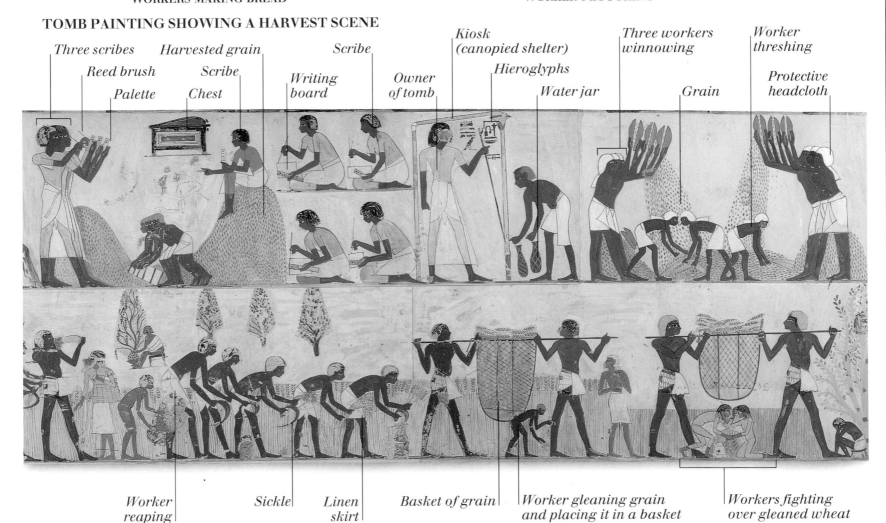

Three scribes

Reed brush

Palette

Harvested grain

Scribe

Chest

Writing board

Scribe

Owner of tomb

Kiosk (canopied shelter)

Hieroglyphs

Water jar

Three workers winnowing

Grain

Worker threshing

Protective headcloth

Worker reaping

Sickle

Linen skirt

Basket of grain

Worker gleaning grain and placing it in a basket

Workers fighting over gleaned wheat

13

Egypt: death and the afterlife

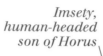

THE ANCIENT EGYPTIANS BELIEVED that when they died they journeyed to the world of the dead and enjoyed an afterlife. Every person had a spirit that survived death if the body was embalmed to preserve it. During embalming, the internal organs were removed and usually placed in four canopic jars, each of which was guarded by a son of the god Horus (Horus guided the deceased through the world of the dead). Even when the jars were not used to hold organs, dummy jars were put in the tombs as charms. The body was treated with preservatives and wrapped in linen bandages, among which were placed protective charms or amulets, such as the eye of Horus (also called the wedjat eye). The bandaged body – known as a mummy – was then fitted with a face mask and placed inside a mummy case, which was painted with religious images and texts, such as scenes from the Book of the Dead (a collection of texts and spells to help the deceased in the afterlife). Mummies were often buried with provisions for the world of the dead; these ranged from food and furniture to shabti figures – models of labourers who would work in the next world on behalf of the deceased.

SHABTI BOX

Imsety, human-headed son of Horus

Shabti figure

Lid

Painted wooden box

Lid

Priestess Henutmehit, owner of shabti box

Shabti figure

Duamutef, jackal-headed son of Horus

Offerings to gods

MUMMY CASE

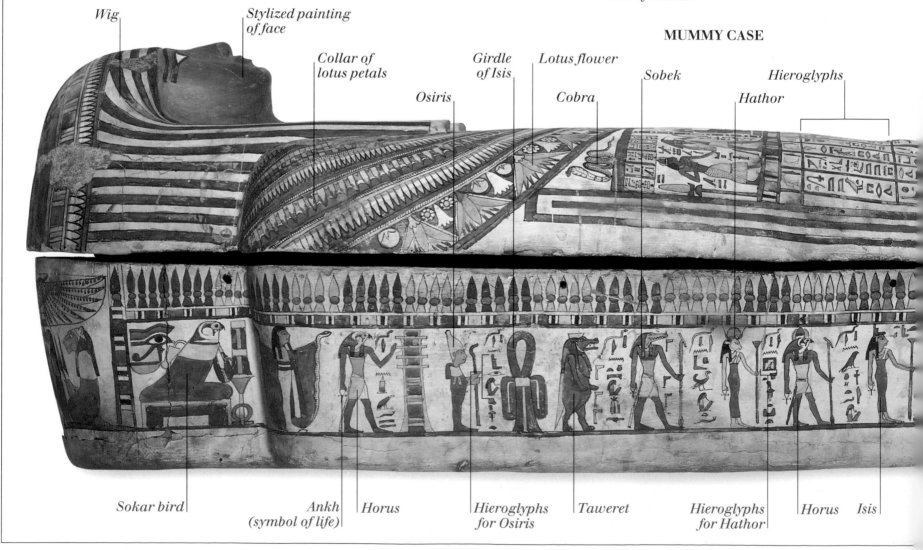

Wig

Stylized painting of face

Collar of lotus petals

Girdle of Isis

Lotus flower

Sobek

Hieroglyphs

Osiris

Cobra

Hathor

Sokar bird

Ankh (symbol of life)

Horus

Hieroglyphs for Osiris

Taweret

Hieroglyphs for Hathor

Horus

Isis

EPINETRON (LEG PROTECTOR)

Section covering thigh

Section covering knee

Wool

Woman preparing wool

Wool being dyed or washed

Stool

Jar

Wool drying

Wool

Woman's face

PYXIS (POT FOR PERFUMES OR COSMETICS)

Handle

Wool

Woman preparing textiles

Lid

Himation (cloak)

Wool

Chiton (tunic)

VASE SHOWING A SYMPOSIUM (BANQUET)

Wreath

Guest

Lyre

Couch

Cushion

Decorative motif

Double pipes

Guest

Kylix (drinking cup)

Table

Musician

RHYTON (DRINKING CUP)

Banquet guest

Cushioned couch

Kylix (drinking cup)

Handle

Ram's head

KYLIX (DRINKING CUP)

Kylix

Musician

Double pipes

Musician

Lyre

Banquet guest

Handle

Rome: the army

HORSEHEAD ARMOUR

ROME WAS ONE OF A NUMBER of towns under Etruscan influence until 509 BC, when the Romans overthrew their kings and established a republic. Over the following centuries, Rome expanded to become the dominant power in the Mediterranean region. In 27 BC, after a period of unrest and civil war, Augustus became the first Roman emperor. He restored peace and for the next 450 years Rome and its vast territories were governed by emperors. Rome's success was founded on its well-organized army. The army was divided into legions of 5,000 soldiers, who were called legionaries. A legion consisted of ten cohorts, each with six centuries comprising about 80 men. The legions were backed up by auxiliary troops – cavalry and infantry units often composed of non-Roman citizens. A legionary's armour included a helmet and a cuirass that protected the upper body. A legionary's usual weapons were a spear, a short sword, and a dagger. The Romans celebrated their military successes with parades and depicted them in sculptured reliefs. For example, reliefs showing the conquest of Romania, then called Dacia, adorn Trajan's column in Rome.

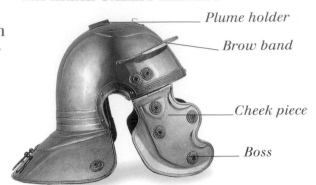

Plume holder

Brow band

Cheek piece

Boss

CUIRASS (LORICA SEGMENTATA)

Collar plate *Buckle* *Shoulder plate*

Embossed rivet

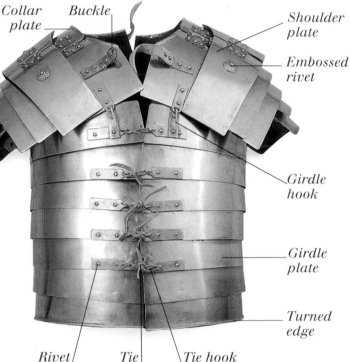

Girdle hook

Girdle plate

Turned edge

Rivet *Tie* *Tie hook*

SWORD AND SCABBARD

Emperor Tiberius receiving his nephew Germanicus

Portrait of Emperor Tiberius

Shrine

Legion's eagle standard

Blade

RELIEF FROM THE BASE OF THE COLUMN OF ANTONINUS PIUS SHOWING A CAVALRY PARADE

Standard bearer *Legion's standard* *Cuirass* *Regimental horse blanket*

Standard or banner

Legionary

Spear

Cavalryman

Military palla (cloak)

Plumed helmet

Shield

Cavalryman

Legionaries

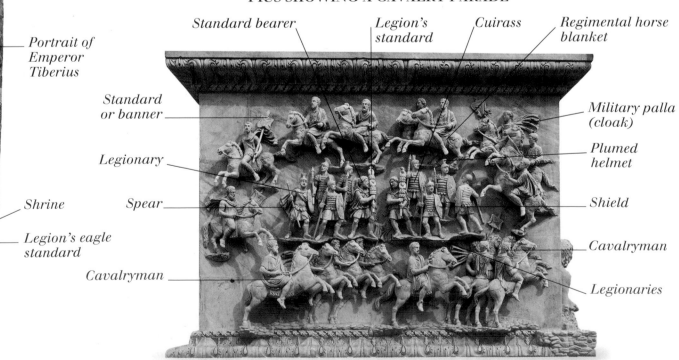

SECTION OF TRAJAN'S COLUMN SHOWING SCENES
FROM THE CAMPAIGN AGAINST DACIA

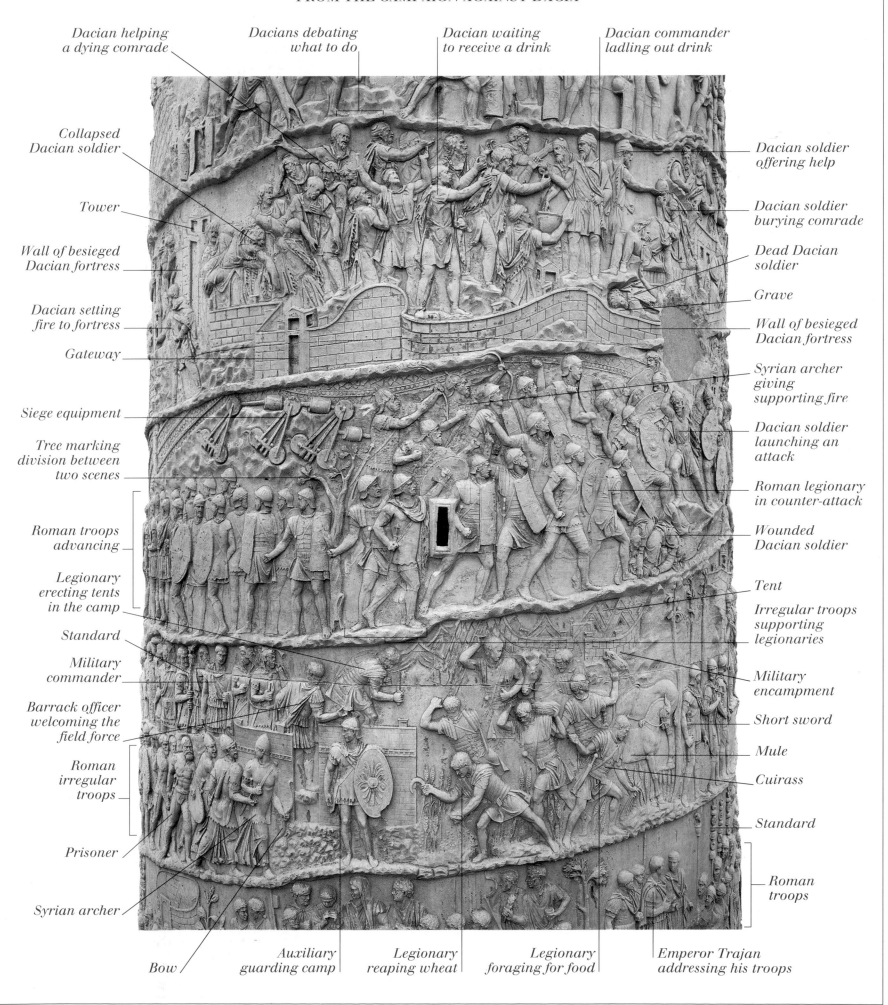

Dacian helping
a dying comrade

Dacians debating
what to do

Dacian waiting
to receive a drink

Dacian commander
ladling out drink

Collapsed
Dacian soldier

Dacian soldier
offering help

Tower

Dacian soldier
burying comrade

Wall of besieged
Dacian fortress

Dead Dacian
soldier

Grave

Dacian setting
fire to fortress

Wall of besieged
Dacian fortress

Gateway

Syrian archer
giving
supporting fire

Siege equipment

Dacian soldier
launching an
attack

Tree marking
division between
two scenes

Roman legionary
in counter-attack

Roman troops
advancing

Wounded
Dacian soldier

Legionary
erecting tents
in the camp

Tent

Irregular troops
supporting
legionaries

Standard

Military
commander

Military
encampment

Barrack officer
welcoming the
field force

Short sword

Roman
irregular
troops

Mule

Cuirass

Standard

Prisoner

Syrian archer

Roman
troops

Bow

Auxiliary
guarding camp

Legionary
reaping wheat

Legionary
foraging for food

Emperor Trajan
addressing his troops

Rome: architecture

BY THE FIRST CENTURY, Rome had become the largest city in the western world, with more than a million inhabitants. The city steadily acquired an array of magnificent civic buildings – temples, stadiums, and public baths – designed to reflect the might of the Roman Empire. Two of the most impressive monuments in Rome were the Colosseum, a huge amphitheatre seating 50,000 people; and the Pantheon, a temple that had the largest dome in the world at the time. Both these monuments were partly built in concrete, a widely used Roman building material, and they had typical Roman architectural features. The Colosseum had decorative columns and arches, and the Pantheon had a massive dome and an elaborate, marble-veneered interior. The Romans built extensively throughout their empire, which extended from the Atlantic Ocean to the Black Sea at its greatest extent. They laid out new cities on a grid plan, and constructed aqueducts – water channels raised on arches in some places – to provide them with a water supply. By the third century, most cities were defended by walls with fortified gateways, of which the Porta Nigra is an example.

LIBRARY OF CELSUS, EPHESUS, TURKEY

MAP OF ANCIENT ROME

- Stadium of Domitian
- Pantheon
- Gardens of Lucullus
- Camp of the Praetorian Guard
- Forum of Trajan
- Forum Romanum
- Aqueduct
- Baths of Trajan
- Colosseum
- Imperial palace
- Baths of Caracalla
- Circus Maximus
- River Tiber

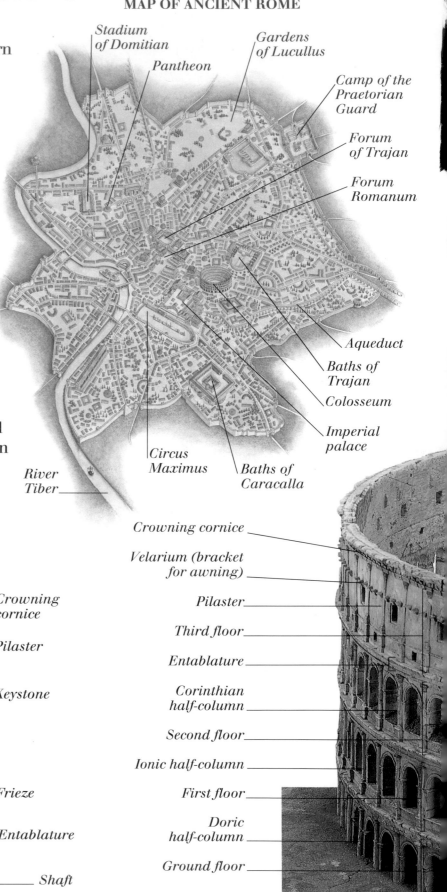

- Crowning cornice
- Velarium (bracket for awning)
- Pilaster
- Third floor
- Entablature
- Corinthian half-column
- Second floor
- Ionic half-column
- First floor
- Doric half-column
- Ground floor

PORTA NIGRA, TRIER, GERMANY, c.180

- Semicircular tower
- Semicircular tower lacking original top storey
- Round-arched window
- Parapet
- Crowning cornice
- Pilaster
- Keystone
- Frieze
- Entablature
- Shaft
- Attached column
- Lobby
- Round arch
- Entrance to town
- Capital
- Base

THE PANTHEON, ROME, c.118–128

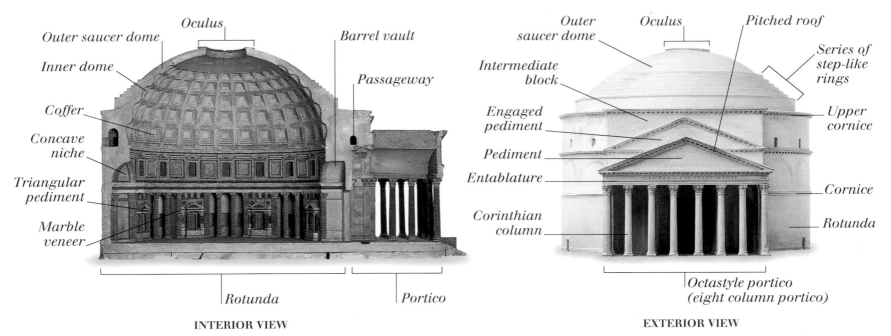

INTERIOR VIEW

Oculus
Outer saucer dome
Inner dome
Coffer
Concave niche
Triangular pediment
Marble veneer
Barrel vault
Passageway
Rotunda
Portico

EXTERIOR VIEW

Outer saucer dome
Oculus
Pitched roof
Intermediate block
Series of step-like rings
Engaged pediment
Upper cornice
Pediment
Entablature
Cornice
Corinthian column
Rotunda
Octastyle portico (eight column portico)

THE COLOSSEUM (FLAVIAN AMPHITHEATRE), ROME, 72–80

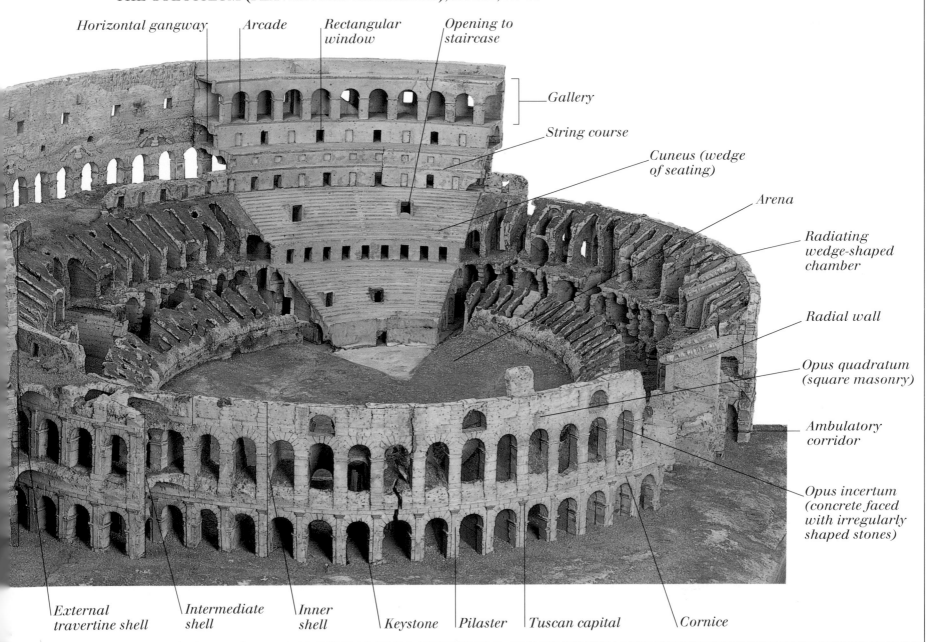

Horizontal gangway
Arcade
Rectangular window
Opening to staircase
Gallery
String course
Cuneus (wedge of seating)
Arena
Radiating wedge-shaped chamber
Radial wall
Opus quadratum (square masonry)
Ambulatory corridor
Opus incertum (concrete faced with irregularly shaped stones)
External travertine shell
Intermediate shell
Inner shell
Keystone
Pilaster
Tuscan capital
Cornice

Rome: imperial trade and prosperity

THE ROMAN EMPIRE created conditions that allowed trade and prosperity to grow in the Mediterranean region and much of Europe. The empire imposed stability on the area, removed internal barriers to trade, and created both a single currency and standard weights and measures. Rome itself was the hub of the trade network: like all the large cities of the empire, it was obliged to import food, most notably grain from Egypt and North Africa. More exotic imports included wild animals from Britain, Germany, and the Near East (for the circus), and silks and spices from the Far East. In return, artisans in Rome produced jewellery, fine pots, and bronze jugs to be sold abroad. The most economical means of transport for trade goods was by ship, across the sea and along the great rivers, such as the Rhine. Wine, olive oil, and fish paste were transported in pottery storage jars called amphorae, which could be packed tightly in the hold of a ship. As settlements and military camps developed in different provinces of the empire, the Roman way of life spread, creating an increased demand for Roman goods such as wine, fine pottery, and glass. In time, cities and regions outside Rome began to produce their own goods; Cologne in Germany, for example, became famous for its glassware.

GOLD EARRINGS

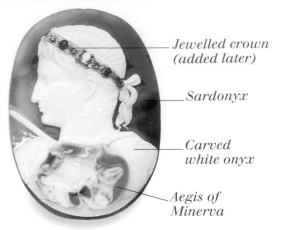

CAMEO SHOWING EMPEROR AUGUSTUS

Jewelled crown (added later)

Sardonyx

Carved white onyx

Aegis of Minerva

EXAMPLES OF ROMAN COINS

Laurel crown

As, the smallest bronze coin

Head of emperor

Aureus, gold coin worth 100 sestertii

Sestertius, bronze coin worth four asses

Denarius, silver coin worth 16 asses

BRONZE STEELYARD AND WEIGHT

Hook for hanging the steelyard

Arm inscribed with scale

Acorn-shaped weight

Hook for weighing objects in bags

STONE RELIEF SHOWING SHOP SCENE

Embroidered material

Cover

Cushion

Tiled roof

Corinthian column

Shop assistant

Shopkeeper

Attendants

Curved lip

INLAID BRONZE LIBATION JUG

Inlaid decoration

Border   _Figure_   _Moulded decoration_

Arch

Plant   _Bird_

SAMIAN WARE BOWL

Inscription

Chariot race

GLASS BEAKER

Narrowed neck

Handle

Narrowed base

WINE AMPHORA (STORAGE JAR)

CORBITA (ROMAN TRADING SHIP)

Masthead

Main sail

Mast

Yard

Main brace

Fore sail

Heraldic device

Yard

Eye

Fore mast

Fore stay

Ladder

Tiller

Brace

Poop deck

Helmsman

Anchor

Poop deck house

Prow

Ladder

Deck

Deck beam

Planking   _Cargo hold_   _Main sheet_   _Rudder_

37

The Maya

BALL-COURT MARKER

THE MAYAN CIVILIZATION was one of the major civilizations of the ancient Americas. Reaching its height between about 250 and 900, this sophisticated civilization spread across much of Central America. There, great Mayan cities were dominated by stone palaces and by temple-topped, stepped pyramids. Mayan society was hierarchically organized, and the ruler and other important people, such as nobles and warriors, wore colourful feathered head-dresses that distinguished them from the rest of the population. Mayan life was dominated by deities that were linked with aspects of the natural world, such as the Sun, Moon, and rain. The daily "death" of the Sun at nightfall and its "rebirth" at daybreak were re-enacted in a symbolic battle called the ball-game, in which two teams propelled a hard rubber ball around a special court without using their hands or feet. The losing team was often put to death. Human sacrifice and other bloodletting rituals were important to the Maya, who believed that the gods required human blood for sustenance. The Maya were expert astronomers and mathematicians, and devised a complex calendar. They also used a representational form of writing made up of pictographic symbols known as glyphs.

VESSEL DECORATION SHOWING THE BALL-GAME

Yoke for hitting ball · Ball-game player · Hummingbird head-dress · Glyph · Ball-game player

Protection for one foot · Protection for one arm · Rubber ball · Black body paint · Protection for one knee · Padded clothing

POTTERY FIGURINES

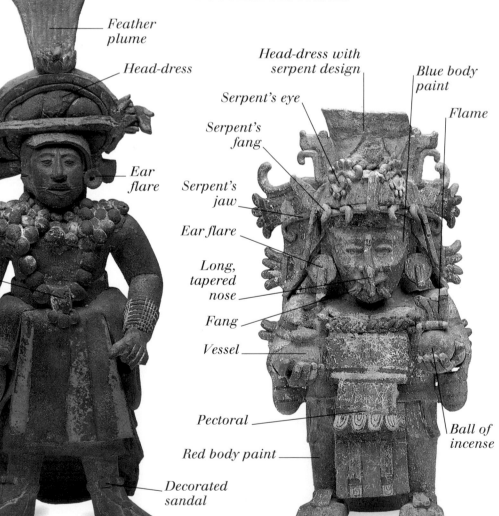

Feather plume

Head-dress

Ear flare

Jade necklace

Masquette

Jade bracelet

Head-dress with serpent design

Serpent's eye

Serpent's fang

Serpent's jaw

Ear flare

Long, tapered nose

Fang

Vessel

Pectoral

Red body paint

Blue body paint

Flame

Ball of incense

Helmet

Ear flare

Protective armband

Yoke for hitting ball

Padded clothing

Sandal

Decorated sandal

BALL-GAME PLAYER

NOBLEMAN

CHAC, GOD OF RAIN

LINTEL FROM CITY OF YAXCHILAN SHOWING BLOODLETTING RITE

Glyphs for "he is letting blood"

Unidentified glyph

Glyph stating he was 60–80 years old

Glyphs for "Shield Jaguar, the captor of Ah Ahaual"

Glyph showing date on Mayan calendar equivalent to 28 October 709

Glyph for "Lord of Yaxchilan"

Shrunken head of sacrificial victim

Flame

Rope collar worn for bloodletting rite

Torch

Plume

Tlaloc head-dress for bloodletting and sacrificial rites

Shield Jaguar (name of king)

Finely woven, pleated cape

Flower tassel

Bead necklace

Barbed rope pushed through tongue

Sun-god pectoral

Glyph for "she is letting blood"

Ear flare

Glyph for unidentified name

Dotted scrolls indicating blood

Sun-god brooch

Glyph for "Lady Xoc"

Jade mosaic collar

Glyph for "Lady Batab"

Mosaic cuff

Lady Xoc, wife of Shield Jaguar

Jade ornament

Thorn

Rope

Stingray spine

Decorated fringed cloak

Jaguar-pelt high-back sandal

Blood-spotted paper

Woven basket to collect blood

Diamond-patterned garment

The Aztecs

DURING THE 15TH CENTURY, the Aztecs came to dominate large parts of Mexico, until they in turn were conquered by the Spaniards in 1521. Military prowess was important in the Aztec state, whose self-styled Warriors of the Sun waged wars to subjugate neighbouring lands and to obtain tribute goods from them. Soldiers were rewarded with elaborate costumes to show how many captives they had taken, the most successful becoming Jaguar or Eagle Knights. The Aztec capital, Tenochtitlan, was built on a lake. At the centre of the city was the Great Temple, built around older versions in onion-like layers, with a place of sacrifice at the top. Here some captives had their hearts cut out as offerings to the god Tlaloc and to sustain the god Huitzilopochtli in his daily battle to avert the end of the world – the Aztecs believed that they lived in the fifth and final world creation. Captives who were sacrificed to Xipe Totec, god of springtime, were skinned alive and priests then wore the victim's skin to symbolize renewal. The Aztecs were also expert astronomers, had a complex calendar system, and made beautiful manuscripts, such as the Codex Mendoza commissioned by the Spaniards.

STATUE OF XIPE TOTEC, GOD OF SPRINGTIME

AZTEC SUN STONE

4-Ehecatl, date of destruction of a previous world

Mask of earth monster or sun god

4-Ocelotl, date of destruction of a previous world

Claw

4-Atl, date of destruction of a previous world

4-Quiahuitl, date of destruction of a previous world

Glyph for one day

Band showing the 20 days of the Aztec month

Two confronting heads of Xiuhcoatl, the celestial serpent

GREAT TEMPLE AT TENOCHTITLAN

Temple of Huitzilopochtli, Aztec patron god

Frieze of human skulls

Temple of Tlaloc, god of rain

Sacrificial stone

Incense burner

Temple built c.1500

Temple built 1469

Temple built 1454

Chacmool figure, for holding the hearts of sacrificial victims

Temple built 1431

Temple built 1390

Steps down which victims' bodies were thrown

Brazier

Serpent head

Brazier

Serpent head

Possible nobles' or priests' residences

Stone showing the goddess Coyolxauhqui

Serpent head

40

CODEX MENDOZA

FOLIO SHOWING HONOURS AWARDED TO WARRIORS

Costume for priest who has captured one enemy

Captive

Costume for priest who has captured five enemies

Costume for priest who has captured four enemies

Glyph for "Cuauhnochteuctli. Officer"

Glyph for "Tlillancalqui. Officer"

Glyph for "Tlacochcalcatl"

Glyph for "Tezcacoacatl"

Costume for priest who has captured two enemies

Costume for priest who has captured three enemies

Jaguar mask

Costume for priest who has captured six enemies

Glyph for "Ezhuahuancatl. Officer"

Glyph for "Atempanecatl. Officer"

Glyph for "Tocuiltecatl"

Glyph for "Ticociahuacatl"

Spanish explanatory text

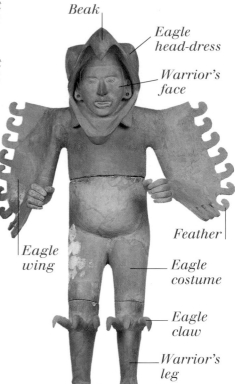

LIFE-SIZE TERRACOTTA FIGURE OF AN EAGLE WARRIOR

Beak

Eagle head-dress

Warrior's face

Feather

Eagle costume

Eagle claw

Warrior's leg

Eagle wing

FOLIO SHOWING TRIBUTE PAID BY 14 TOWNS TO MONTEZUMA

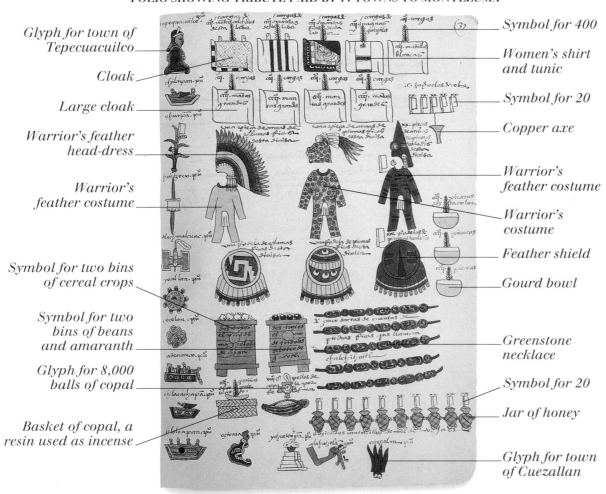

Glyph for town of Tepecuacuilco

Cloak

Large cloak

Warrior's feather head-dress

Warrior's feather costume

Symbol for two bins of cereal crops

Symbol for two bins of beans and amaranth

Glyph for 8,000 balls of copal

Basket of copal, a resin used as incense

Symbol for 400

Women's shirt and tunic

Symbol for 20

Copper axe

Warrior's feather costume

Warrior's costume

Feather shield

Gourd bowl

Greenstone necklace

Symbol for 20

Jar of honey

Glyph for town of Cuezallan

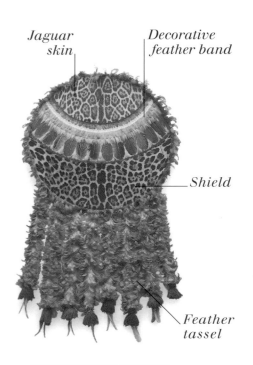

RECONSTRUCTION OF A WARRIOR'S FEATHER SHIELD

Jaguar skin

Decorative feather band

Shield

Feather tassel

Andean civilizations

THE ANDES REGION OF SOUTH AMERICA – a long mountainous area running parallel to the Pacific Ocean – was inhabited by many civilizations, including the Moche, Chimu, and Inca. Although the Andean civilizations occupied different parts of the region at various periods from the 13th century BC until the 16th century AD, they shared some characteristics. Common aspects included crafts, such as elaborate goldwork, pottery, and textiles; the use of the llama as a beast of burden and a source of wool and meat; well-trained armies; similar beliefs and deities, such as a Sun and jaguar god; a reverence for mountain-tops; and the practice of human sacrifice. The Moche, famed for their pottery, flourished during the first six centuries AD. They were also skilled engineers and built a network of roads over mountainous terrain that gave them good control over their subject territories. The Chimu, who were famed for their goldwork, ruled northern Peru from about 800 until their defeat by the Incas in 1476. The Incas built towns, bridges, and new roads, and used the skills of subject craftspeople to produce fine textiles and goldwork. The Inca Empire was the largest ever seen in the Andes, but it fell to the Spanish conquerors less than 100 years later.

INCA GOLD LLAMA

INCA UNQO (TUNIC)

Chequered motif

Slit for neck

T'okapu band with important symbols

Patterns give information about the wearer

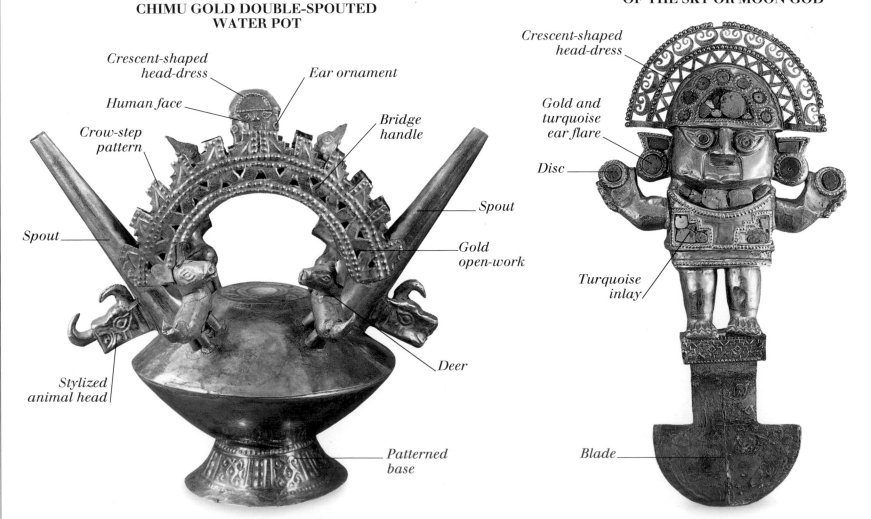

CHIMU GOLD DOUBLE-SPOUTED WATER POT

Crescent-shaped head-dress

Ear ornament

Human face

Crow-step pattern

Bridge handle

Spout

Spout

Gold open-work

Deer

Stylized animal head

Patterned base

CHIMU TUMI (CEREMONIAL KNIFE) OF THE SKY OR MOON GOD

Crescent-shaped head-dress

Gold and turquoise ear flare

Disc

Turquoise inlay

Blade

MOCHE POTTERY

POT SHOWING MOUNTAIN SCENE

God, possibly Ai Apec

Sacred mountain

Snake with ears, enemy of Ai Apec

Mountain peak

Ai Apec's assistant

Ai Apec's assistant

Warrior

Seated figure

Snake

Plant

Figure, possibly a sacrificial victim

Bird

POT SHOWING TWO FIGURES

Feline deity

Fang

Paw

Seated figure, possibly a prisoner

Claw

POT SHOWING MESSENGERS

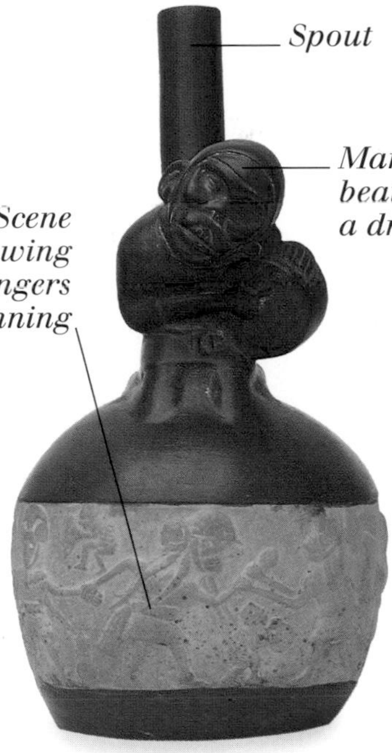

Spout

Man beating a drum

Scene showing messengers running

WARRIOR-SHAPED POT

Helmet

Spiral-patterned shirt

Weapon

Shield

North American civilizations

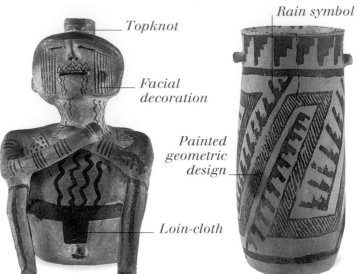

IN SOUTHWESTERN NORTH AMERICA, three prehistoric civilizations – the Hohokam, the Mogollon, and the Anasazi – flourished between the first century and the 15th century. All three were influenced by the civilizations of Mexico. The Hohokam were skilled farmers who irrigated the plains of southern Arizona. They were the first people to develop a decorative technique that used cactus juice, a weak acid, to etch designs on shells. The Mogollon were based in the mountains of New Mexico, where they lived in pit-houses. They produced a distinctive pottery, known as Mimbres pottery, which was often ritually punctured, possibly to allow the spirit of the owner to escape the body at death. In about 1300 the Mogollon civilization was absorbed by the more sophisticated Anasazi civilization, which dominated the region where the states of Utah, Arizona, Colorado, and New Mexico meet. The Anasazis' great achievement was their pueblos – complex settlements composed of rows of adjoining rooms, often several storeys high. The largest, Pueblo Bonito in Chaco Canyon, New Mexico, contained over 800 rooms. Other pueblos such as Mesa Verde were built under the canyon cliffs. Each pueblo had a number of kivas – half-underground circular chambers where the men of the community would meet and perform ceremonies. The network of roads radiating from Chaco Canyon suggests it was an important trading centre.

HOHOKAM ETCHED SHELL

Topknot

Facial decoration

Loin-cloth

ANASAZI POTTERY EFFIGY JAR

Rain symbol

Painted geometric design

ANASAZI POT

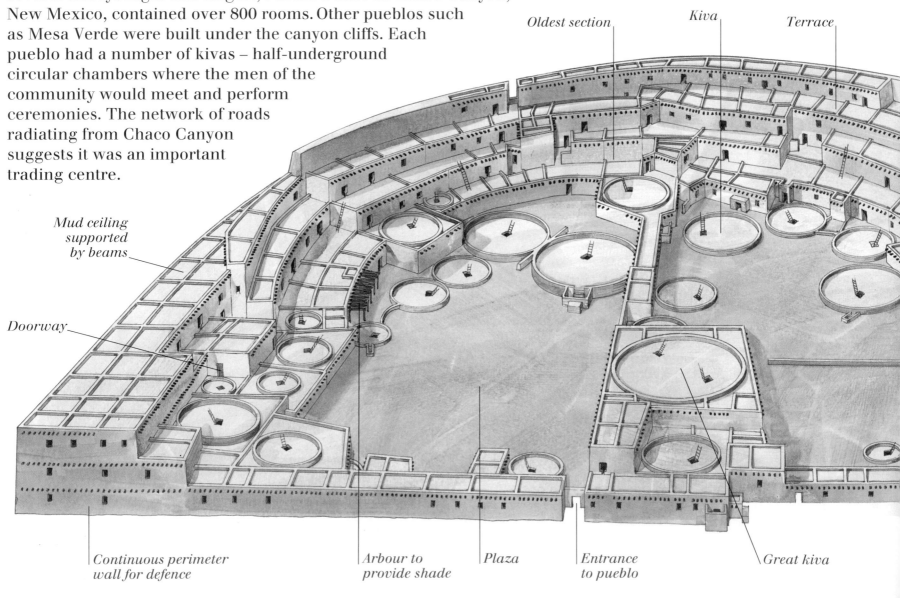

Oldest section

Kiva

Terrace

Mud ceiling supported by beams

Doorway

Continuous perimeter wall for defence

Arbour to provide shade

Plaza

Entrance to pueblo

Great kiva

ANASAZI PUEBLO AT MESA VERDE

Cliff wall

Support beams

Watchtower

T-shaped doorway

Kiva

Apartment

Kiva

Steps

MIMBRES POTTERY

Decorated headband

Male figure

Facial decoration

Necklace

Female figure

Ritual puncture

Armband

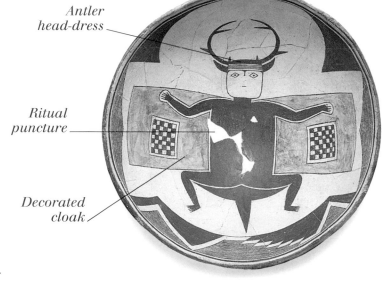

BOWL SHOWING A MAN AND A WOMAN

Antler head-dress

Ritual puncture

Decorated cloak

BOWL SHOWING A MAN IN DEER DRESS

PUEBLO BONITO, AN ANASAZI SETTLEMENT

Stone wall

Housing for macaws, kept for their valuable feathers

Ladder for entrance to kiva

Typical apartment comprising a living room and two storerooms

Pinewood frame for roof

Kiva

Room in apartment

Circular bench

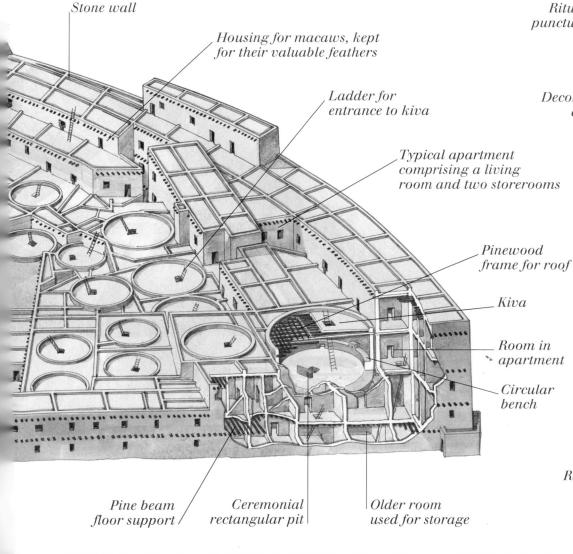

Pine beam floor support

Ceremonial rectangular pit

Older room used for storage

Geometric design

Rabbit head

BOWL WITH A RABBIT-HEAD DESIGN

India: Buddhism

THE BUDDHIST RELIGION was founded in northern India about 2,500 years ago by a prince named Siddhartha Gautama. He left his wife, family, and a luxurious palace for a life of contemplation and wandering in search of spiritual truth. After years spent exploring and considering different spiritual paths, Siddhartha Gautama found enlightenment while meditating under a pipal tree at Bodh Gaya. From this time on, Siddhartha Gautama became known as the Buddha, the Enlightened One. The Buddha was a great spiritual teacher and when he died, in about 480 BC, his followers took his teachings to other parts of India. Later, Buddhism reached Southeast Asia and the Far East, and eventually became known throughout the world. The Buddha's followers preserved ashes from his cremation as relics and placed them in special containers called reliquaries. These were often deposited in large mound-like structures known as stupas. One of the great Buddhist stupas was built at Amaravati in southern India. Reliefs showing incidents from the life of the Buddha and other Buddhist subjects covered the stupa and its surrounding railing.

STATUE OF THE BUDDHA

GOLD RELIQUARY

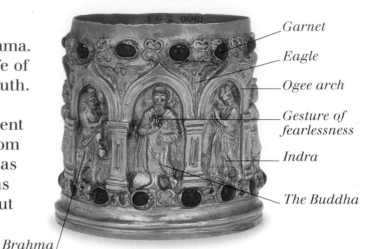

Garnet

Eagle

Ogee arch

Gesture of fearlessness

Indra

The Buddha

Brahma

RELIEF FROM A STUPA, NORTHERN INDIA

Auspicious female figure

Guard

Reliquary

Table

Drona distributing the Buddha's relics

THE STUPA AT AMARAVATI, SOUTHERN INDIA

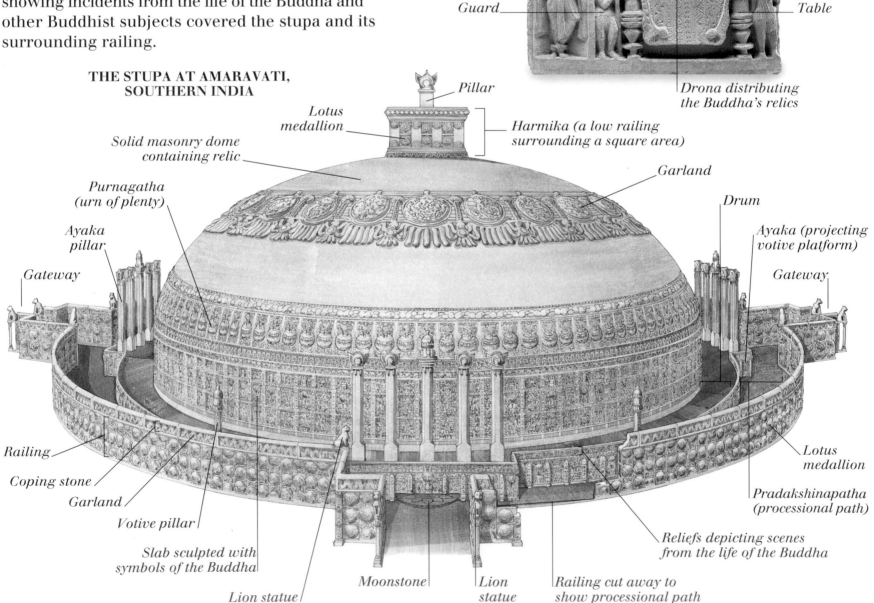

Pillar

Lotus medallion

Solid masonry dome containing relic

Harmika (a low railing surrounding a square area)

Garland

Purnagatha (urn of plenty)

Drum

Ayaka pillar

Ayaka (projecting votive platform)

Gateway

Gateway

Railing

Lotus medallion

Coping stone

Garland

Votive pillar

Pradakshinapatha (processional path)

Reliefs depicting scenes from the life of the Buddha

Slab sculpted with symbols of the Buddha

Moonstone

Lion statue

Lion statue

Railing cut away to show processional path

FRIEZE FROM THE STUPA AT AMARAVATI SHOWING "THE GREAT DEPARTURE"

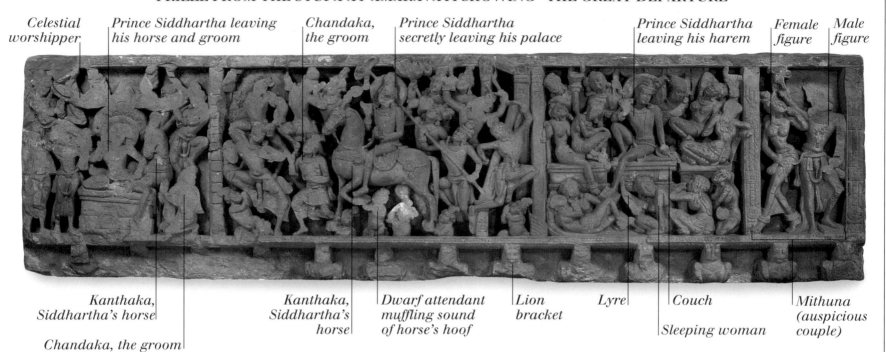

Celestial worshipper

Prince Siddhartha leaving his horse and groom

Chandaka, the groom

Prince Siddhartha secretly leaving his palace

Prince Siddhartha leaving his harem

Female figure

Male figure

Kanthaka, Siddhartha's horse

Chandaka, the groom

Kanthaka, Siddhartha's horse

Dwarf attendant muffling sound of horse's hoof

Lion bracket

Lyre

Couch

Sleeping woman

Mithuna (auspicious couple)

RELIEF FROM THE STUPA AT AMARAVATI SHOWING SCENES FROM THE BIRTH OF THE BUDDHA

Courtier

Throne

Prince Shuddhodana, husband of Queen Maya

Queen Maya

Soothsayer interpreting Queen Maya's dream as the imminent birth of the Buddha

Umbrella indicating presence of the Buddha

Sacred tree

Local tree deity honouring the Buddha

Siddhartha depicted symbolically as a pair of footprints

Queen Maya presenting the child

Offering to the tree deity

Queen Maya dreaming

Earring

Anklet

Sleeping attendant

Sal tree in Lumbini Park

Earring

Siddhartha depicted symbolically as a pair of footprints

Swaddling cloth

Queen Maya giving birth to Siddhartha from her right hip

Attendant

47

India: Hinduism

ONE OF THE MAJOR RELIGIONS of India, Hinduism, developed during the first thousand years AD, although its origins are more ancient. Hinduism is a complex faith and its followers embrace a wide range of beliefs and practices. Most Hindus believe that at death the soul is reborn in another body, a process known as reincarnation. This continues until they finally gain release from the cycle of birth, death, and rebirth, by attaining a state called moksha. Hindus worship a large number of deities, including Shiva, an all-encompassing god, and his elephant-headed son Ganesha, and Vishnu, who is traditionally depicted in one of many incarnations or bodily forms. Female deities include Parvati, Shiva's wife, and Durga, a goddess who is famous for killing a demon in the form of a buffalo. Hindus often worship their deities in magnificent temple complexes built to traditional designs. The temple is the abode of a particular god or goddess, whose image is kept inside a central sanctuary. In major temples the sanctuary is usually surrounded by smaller shrines, and the entire complex is enclosed by a series of richly carved walls and gateways.

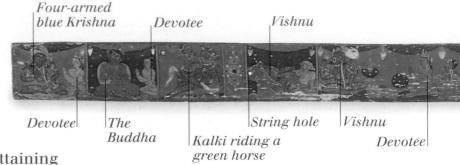

Four-armed blue Krishna — Devotee — Vishnu

Devotee — The Buddha — Kalki riding a green horse — String hole — Vishnu — Devotee

LION PILLAR FROM A TEMPLE

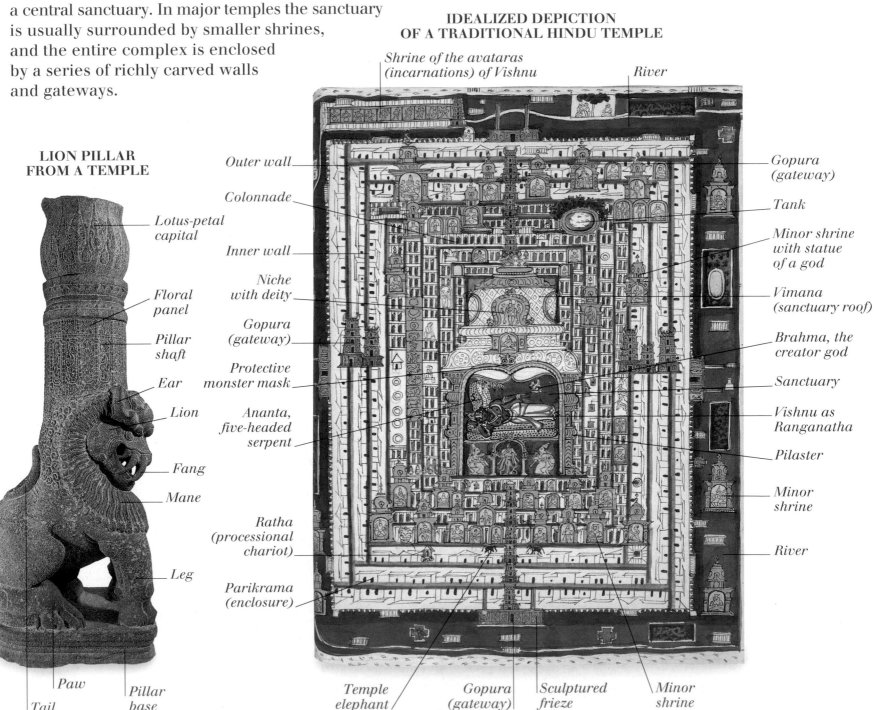

- Lotus-petal capital
- Floral panel
- Pillar shaft
- Ear
- Lion
- Fang
- Mane
- Leg
- Paw
- Pillar base
- Tail

IDEALIZED DEPICTION OF A TRADITIONAL HINDU TEMPLE

- Shrine of the avataras (incarnations) of Vishnu
- River
- Outer wall
- Colonnade
- Inner wall
- Niche with deity
- Gopura (gateway)
- Protective monster mask
- Ananta, five-headed serpent
- Ratha (processional chariot)
- Parikrama (enclosure)
- Gopura (gateway)
- Tank
- Minor shrine with statue of a god
- Vimana (sanctuary roof)
- Brahma, the creator god
- Sanctuary
- Vishnu as Ranganatha
- Pilaster
- Minor shrine
- River
- Temple elephant
- Gopura (gateway)
- Sculptured frieze
- Minor shrine

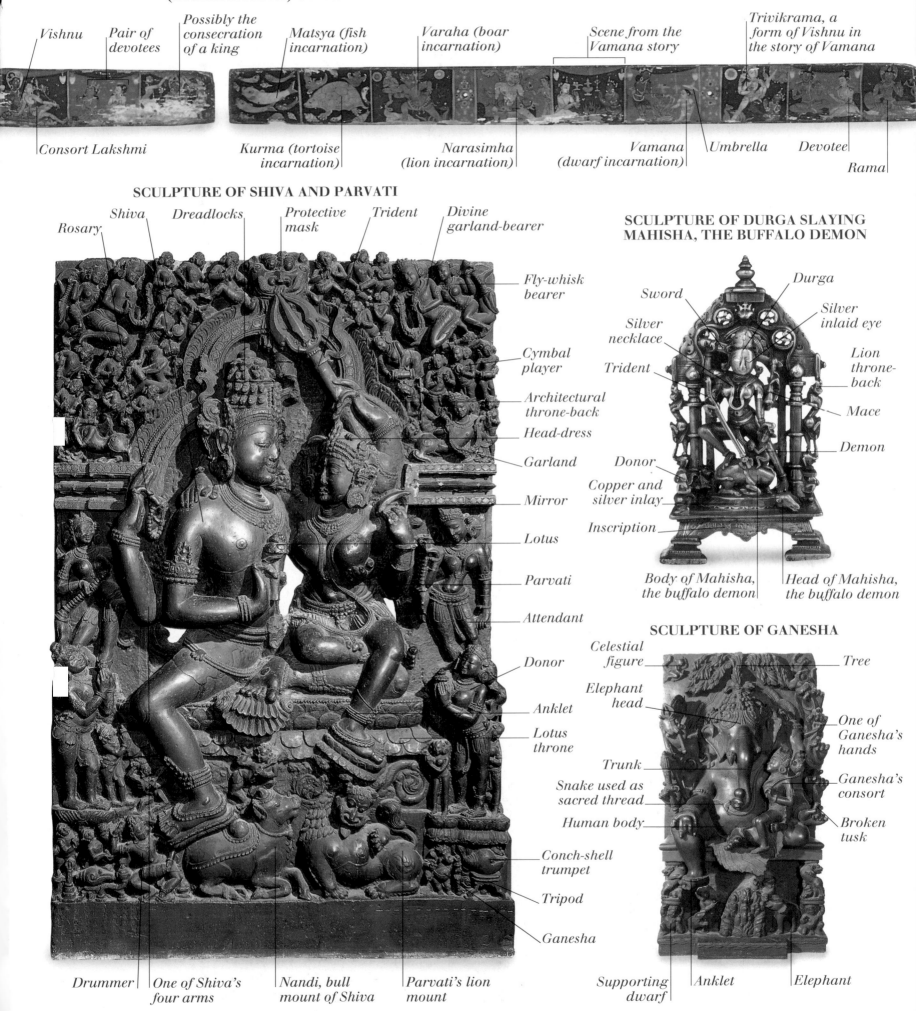

WOODEN BOOK COVERS SHOWING AVATARAS (INCARNATIONS) OF VISHNU

Vishnu

Pair of devotees

Possibly the consecration of a king

Matsya (fish incarnation)

Varaha (boar incarnation)

Scene from the Vamana story

Trivikrama, a form of Vishnu in the story of Vamana

Consort Lakshmi

Kurma (tortoise incarnation)

Narasimha (lion incarnation)

Vamana (dwarf incarnation)

Umbrella

Devotee

Rama

SCULPTURE OF SHIVA AND PARVATI

Rosary

Shiva

Dreadlocks

Protective mask

Trident

Divine garland-bearer

Fly-whisk bearer

Cymbal player

Architectural throne-back

Head-dress

Garland

Mirror

Lotus

Parvati

Attendant

Donor

Anklet

Lotus throne

Conch-shell trumpet

Tripod

Ganesha

Drummer

One of Shiva's four arms

Nandi, bull mount of Shiva

Parvati's lion mount

SCULPTURE OF DURGA SLAYING MAHISHA, THE BUFFALO DEMON

Sword

Durga

Silver necklace

Silver inlaid eye

Trident

Lion throne-back

Mace

Donor

Demon

Copper and silver inlay

Inscription

Body of Mahisha, the buffalo demon

Head of Mahisha, the buffalo demon

SCULPTURE OF GANESHA

Celestial figure

Tree

Elephant head

One of Ganesha's hands

Trunk

Ganesha's consort

Snake used as sacred thread

Human body

Broken tusk

Supporting dwarf

Anklet

Elephant

China: everyday life

CHINA WAS A COLLECTION OF MANY KINGDOMS before it was united in 221 BC by the First Emperor of the Qin Dynasty, who created a strongly centralized state. The Han Dynasty took over from the Qin in 206 BC, and ruled China for about 400 years. During this time, China experienced a period of peace and prosperity. Trade flourished as weights and measures were standardized and good trade routes were established across Asia to the west. The major Chinese export was silk, but merchants also traded bronze and iron utensils for horses, spices, and other goods. Han society was hierarchical; the emperor was the centre of power, and there was a big difference between the living standards of the wealthy landowners and state officials, and the ordinary people. The Han developed a highly organized bureaucracy to administer the empire, which was large in terms of both geographical size and population. The cities were the administrative centres. Chinese imperial cities were laid out according to a rigid plan. The various districts were separated from each other by walls and gatehouses. Watchtowers were a popular feature of Chinese cities. The wealthy lived in mansions built around central courtyards, while the poor lived in simple buildings with walls of rammed earth. Han nobles enjoyed luxurious lives, as is shown by the array of objects found in their tombs, such as lacquerware and silks.

Cloud scroll — Decorated edge — Dedicatory inscription

LACQUERWARE BOWL

Lidded cup — Chopstick — Wine cup — Tray — Food remains — Bowl

LACQUERWARE SET AND TRAY

Finial — Man keeping watch — Decorated eave tile — Dragon-headed bracket arm — Man — Tiled roof — Moat — Fish

TOMB MODEL OF A WATCHTOWER

Tiled roof — Place for cooking pot — Oven

TOMB MODEL OF A STOVE

Topknot — Embroidered border — Hair ornament — Silk robe — Scrolling leaf pattern — Leaf pattern

WOODEN TOMB FIGURES

CERAMIC MODEL OF A GATEHOUSE

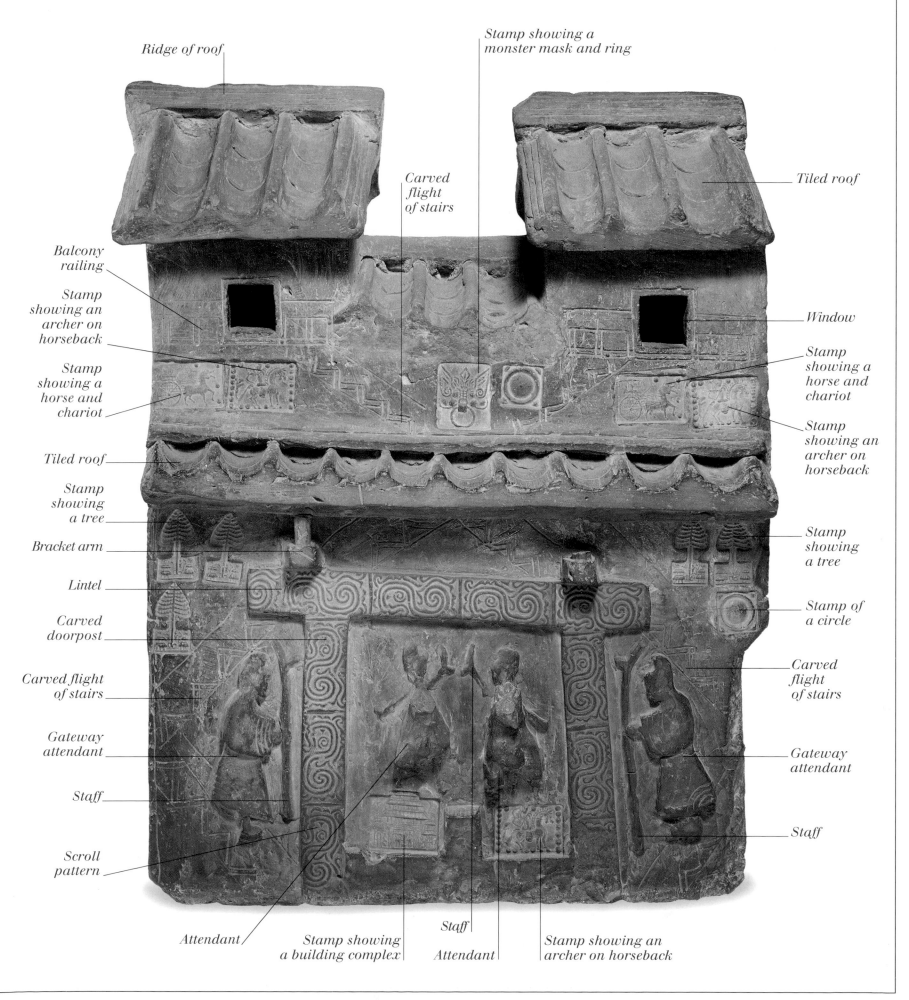

Ridge of roof

Stamp showing a monster mask and ring

Carved flight of stairs

Tiled roof

Balcony railing

Stamp showing an archer on horseback

Window

Stamp showing a horse and chariot

Stamp showing a horse and chariot

Stamp showing an archer on horseback

Tiled roof

Stamp showing a tree

Stamp showing a tree

Bracket arm

Stamp of a circle

Lintel

Carved doorpost

Carved flight of stairs

Carved flight of stairs

Gateway attendant

Gateway attendant

Staff

Staff

Scroll pattern

Attendant

Stamp showing a building complex

Staff

Attendant

Stamp showing an archer on horseback

51

China: ritual and ceremony

THE ANCIENT CHINESE performed a range of religious rituals and ceremonies. The importance of various beliefs changed over time. During the Shang dynasty (c.1600–1027 BC), the Chinese worshipped ancestral spirits by making offerings of wine and food in magnificent bronze vessels. They also practised human sacrifice. Shang diviners used animal bones, known as "oracle bones", to consult the spirits. Bones were heated until cracks appeared, from which the diviners interpreted the spirits' response to questions. The divinations were recorded on the bones, and are among the earliest examples of Chinese writing. The Zhou rulers, who overthrew the Shang in 1027 BC, believed that they had been given the right to rule by heaven. The king's duties included performing rituals to maintain harmony between heaven and the terrestrial world. During the Han dynasty (206 BC–AD 220), nobles were buried in elaborate tombs with objects for use in the afterlife, such as mirrors, which symbolized the universe. A silk tomb banner illustrates the Chinese belief in three realms: an underworld, a terrestrial world, and heaven.

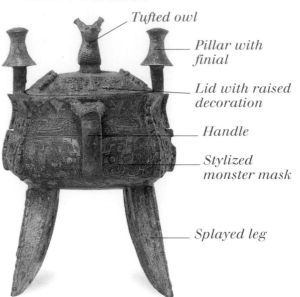

BRONZE RITUAL VESSELS, SHANG DYNASTY

- *Tufted owl*
- *Pillar with finial*
- *Lid with raised decoration*
- *Handle*
- *Stylized monster mask*
- *Splayed leg*

JIA (VESSEL FOR WINE)

- *Knob*
- *Beak-shaped handle*
- *Owl's wing*
- *Raised decoration in the shape of an owl*

ZUN (VESSEL FOR WINE)

RITUAL AXE, ZHOU PERIOD

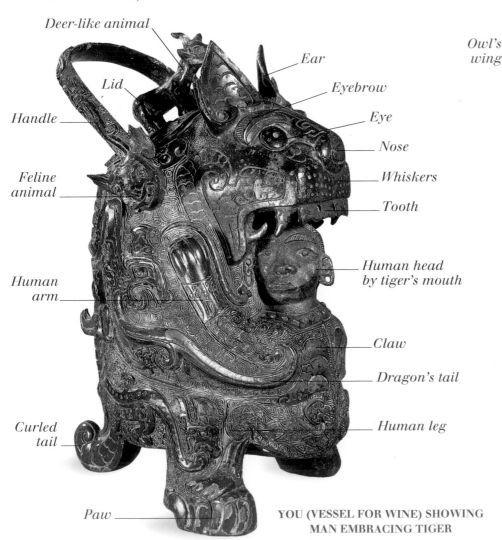

- *Deer-like animal*
- *Ear*
- *Lid*
- *Eyebrow*
- *Handle*
- *Eye*
- *Nose*
- *Whiskers*
- *Feline animal*
- *Tooth*
- *Human head by tiger's mouth*
- *Human arm*
- *Claw*
- *Dragon's tail*
- *Human leg*
- *Curled tail*
- *Paw*

YOU (VESSEL FOR WINE) SHOWING MAN EMBRACING TIGER

- *Inscription*
- *Handle*
- *Snake decoration*
- *Raised boss*
- *Water-buffalo or ox head*

FANG DING (VESSEL FOR FOOD)

DETAIL FROM LOWER SECTION OF SILK BANNER

SILK BANNER SHOWING MYTHOLOGICAL JOURNEY TO HEAVEN, FROM TOMB AT MAWANGDUI, HAN DYNASTY

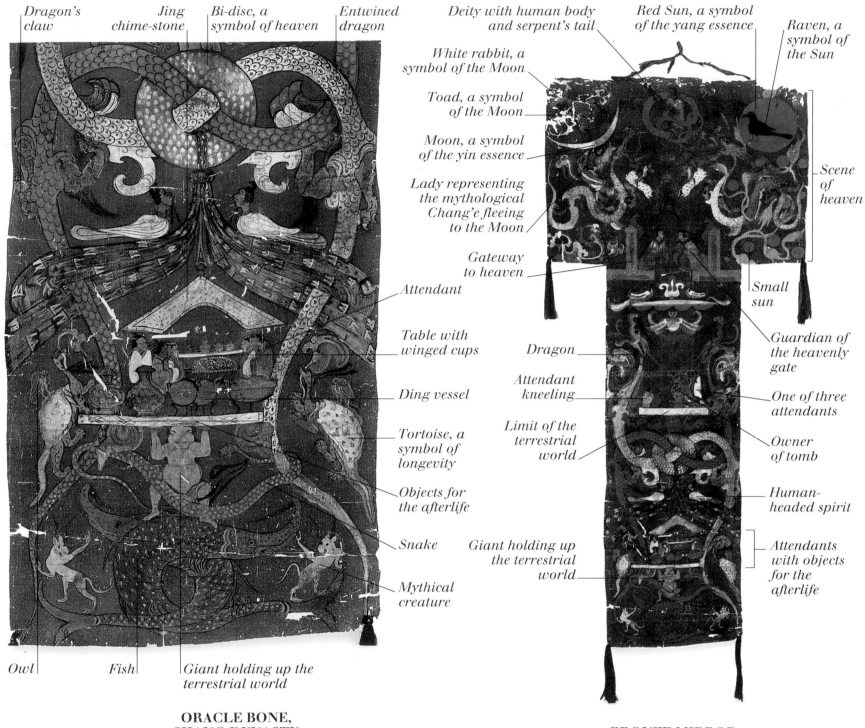

Dragon's claw

Jing chime-stone

Bi-disc, a symbol of heaven

Entwined dragon

Deity with human body and serpent's tail

Red Sun, a symbol of the yang essence

Raven, a symbol of the Sun

White rabbit, a symbol of the Moon

Toad, a symbol of the Moon

Moon, a symbol of the yin essence

Lady representing the mythological Chang'e fleeing to the Moon

Scene of heaven

Attendant

Gateway to heaven

Small sun

Table with winged cups

Dragon

Guardian of the heavenly gate

Ding vessel

Attendant kneeling

One of three attendants

Tortoise, a symbol of longevity

Limit of the terrestrial world

Owner of tomb

Objects for the afterlife

Human-headed spirit

Snake

Giant holding up the terrestrial world

Attendants with objects for the afterlife

Mythical creature

Owl

Fish

Giant holding up the terrestrial world

ORACLE BONE, SHANG DYNASTY

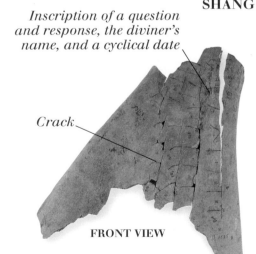

Inscription of a question and response, the diviner's name, and a cyclical date

Burn mark where a hot poker was applied to a carved hole

Crack

Carved hole

FRONT VIEW

BACK VIEW

BRONZE MIRROR, HAN DYNASTY

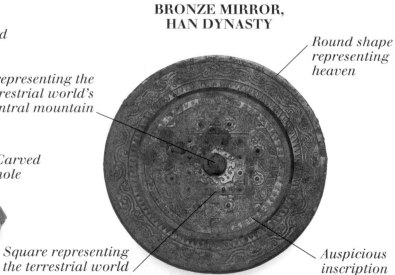

Round shape representing heaven

Boss representing the terrestrial world's central mountain

Square representing the terrestrial world

Auspicious inscription

Japan

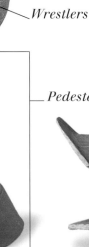

BRONZE DOTAKU BELLS

IN THE FOURTH CENTURY, a number of small Japanese kingdoms were unified under a single ruler. Over the next three centuries, the Japanese imperial line was established, as was Shinto, the native religion. This period, known as the Kofun (Old Tomb) period, was characterized by the building of huge, keyhole-shaped tombs. These tombs were surrounded by haniwa – clay models in the shape of human figures, horses, and other objects. Funerary pottery, called Sue ware, was placed inside the tombs. During the Kofun period, Japan received important cultural influences from China and Korea. Chinese-style writing was adopted by the early sixth century and Buddhism had reached Japan from Korea by the mid-sixth century. Buddhism was popularized by Crown Prince Shotoku (572–622). He encouraged the building of temples and monasteries, such as Hōryū-ji, which he founded in 607 (although this temple was later rebuilt). In time, Buddhist temples came to be regarded as symbols of prestige. Buddhism also introduced new styles of art and architecture. Temples held treasures such as statues of the Buddha and bodhisattvas (holy figures), and sutras, which were scrolls of holy Buddhist texts.

EMPEROR NINTOKU'S TOMB, OSAKA

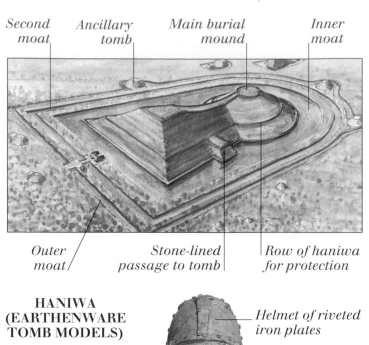

Second moat · Ancillary tomb · Main burial mound · Inner moat

Outer moat · Stone-lined passage to tomb · Row of haniwa for protection

HANIWA (EARTHENWARE TOMB MODELS)

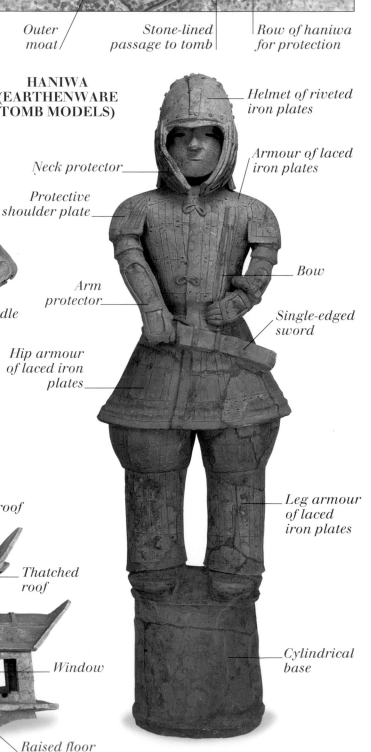

Helmet of riveted iron plates

Neck protector

Armour of laced iron plates

Protective shoulder plate

Arm protector

Bow

Hip armour of laced iron plates

Single-edged sword

Leg armour of laced iron plates

Cylindrical base

HANIWA WARRIOR

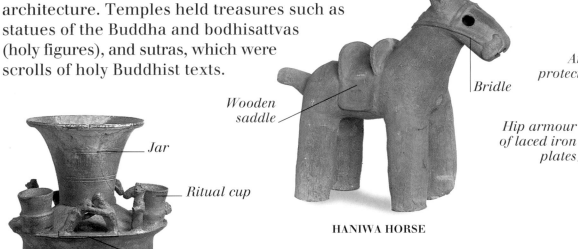

Wooden saddle

Bridle

HANIWA HORSE

Jar

Ritual cup

Wrestlers

Cut-out slot

Pedestal

SUE WARE JAR AND PEDESTAL

Ornamental bargeboard

Hip-and-gable roof

Thatched roof

Window

Raised floor

HANIWA NOBLEMAN'S HOUSE

STATUE OF KANNON, BODHISATTVA OF COMPASSION, FROM HŌRYŪ-JI

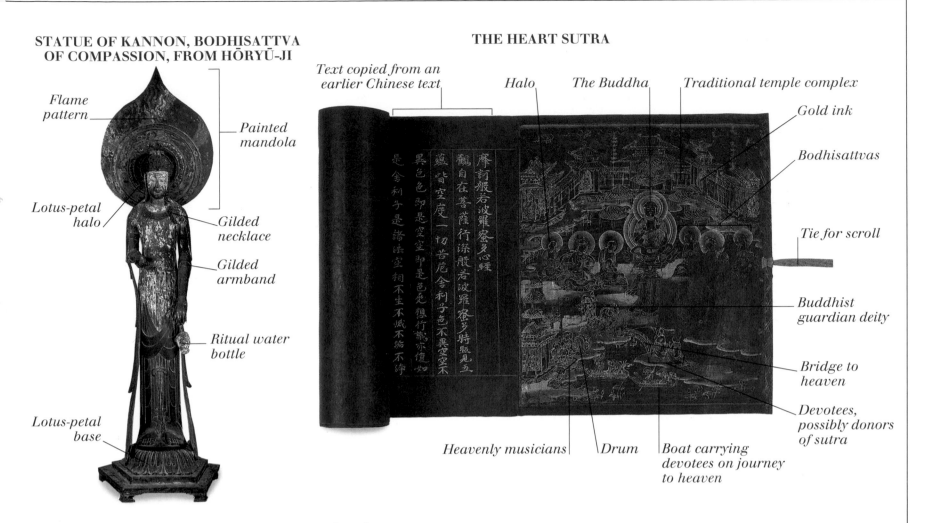

Flame pattern

Painted mandola

Lotus-petal halo

Gilded necklace

Gilded armband

Ritual water bottle

Lotus-petal base

THE HEART SUTRA

Text copied from an earlier Chinese text

Halo

The Buddha

Traditional temple complex

Gold ink

Bodhisattvas

Tie for scroll

Buddhist guardian deity

Bridge to heaven

Devotees, possibly donors of sutra

Heavenly musicians

Drum

Boat carrying devotees on journey to heaven

HŌRYŪ-JI, NARA, AS IT APPEARED IN 607

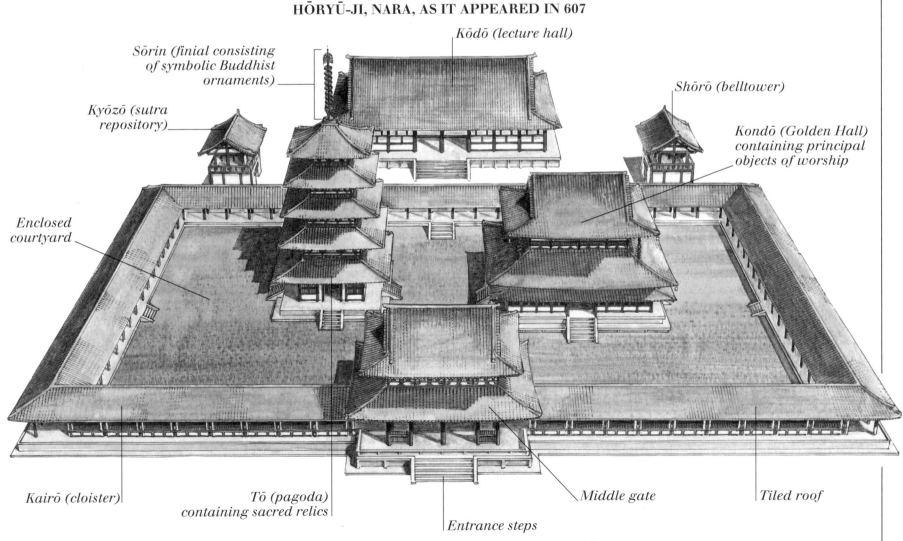

Sōrin (finial consisting of symbolic Buddhist ornaments)

Kōdō (lecture hall)

Shōrō (belltower)

Kyōzō (sutra repository)

Kondō (Golden Hall) containing principal objects of worship

Enclosed courtyard

Kairō (cloister)

Tō (pagoda) containing sacred relics

Middle gate

Tiled roof

Entrance steps

Timelines 1

THE TIMELINES ON THESE PAGES show most of the civilizations
and cultures featured in this book within a chronological
framework. Other cultures, not included in this book, are
also shown to give an indication of what was happening
simultaneously in different parts of the world. The charts
are divided vertically into successive time periods, beginning
with 3500 BC and ending at AD 1600. The civilizations are
shown extending across pages in one of five geographical
regions: the Americas, Australasia and Oceania, the Middle
East and Africa, Europe, and India and the Far East. The
approximate area of each region is shown on the maps
on pages 56 and 58. The principal civilizations within a
particular region – for example, Greece and Rome within
Europe – are distinguished by a colour code, which is also
shown on the maps. The illustrations show some of the
artistic, cultural, and architectural achievements of the
different civilizations.

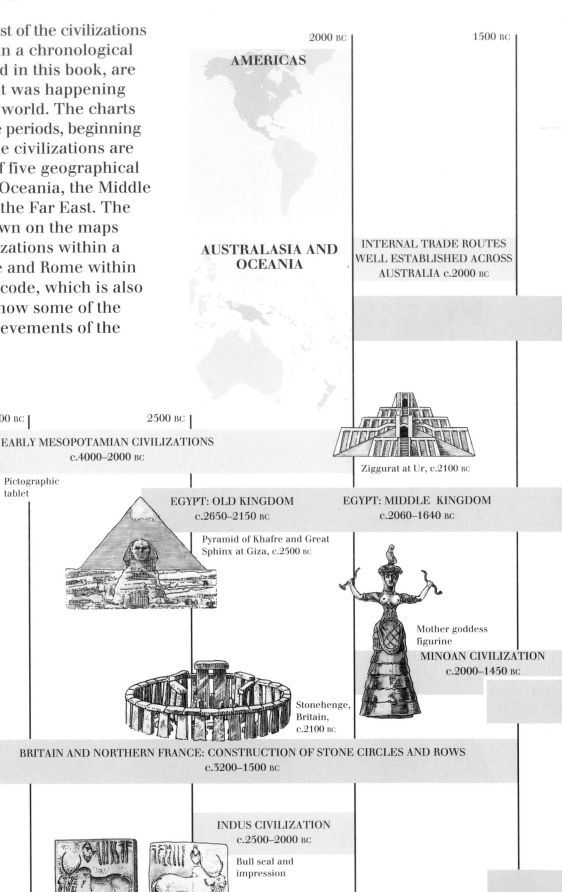

2000 BC   1500 BC

AMERICAS

**AUSTRALASIA AND
OCEANIA**

INTERNAL TRADE ROUTES
WELL ESTABLISHED ACROSS
AUSTRALIA c.2000 BC

3500 BC   3000 BC   2500 BC

**MIDDLE EAST AND
AFRICA**

EARLY MESOPOTAMIAN CIVILIZATIONS
c.4000–2000 BC

Ziggurat at Ur, c.2100 BC

Pictographic
tablet

EGYPT: OLD KINGDOM
c.2650–2150 BC

EGYPT: MIDDLE KINGDOM
c.2060–1640 BC

Pyramid of Khafre and Great
Sphinx at Giza, c.2500 BC

EUROPE

Mother goddess
figurine

MINOAN CIVILIZATION
c.2000–1450 BC

Stonehenge,
Britain,
c.2100 BC

BRITAIN AND NORTHERN FRANCE: CONSTRUCTION OF STONE CIRCLES AND ROWS
c.3200–1500 BC

**INDIA AND THE
FAR EAST**

INDUS CIVILIZATION
c.2500–2000 BC

Bull seal and
impression

3000 BC   2500 BC   2000 BC   1500 BC

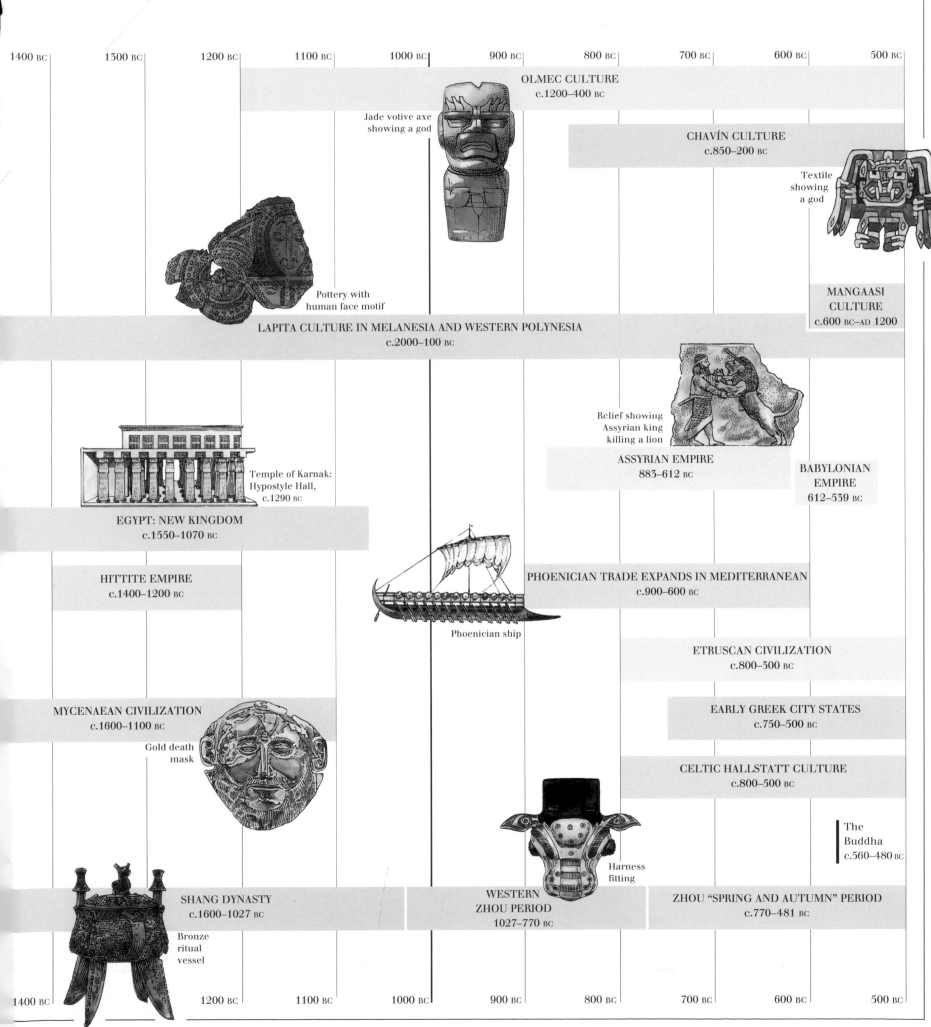

| 1400 BC | 1300 BC | 1200 BC | 1100 BC | 1000 BC | 900 BC | 800 BC | 700 BC | 600 BC | 500 BC |

OLMEC CULTURE
c.1200–400 BC

Jade votive axe
showing a god

CHAVÍN CULTURE
c.850–200 BC

Textile
showing
a god

Pottery with
human face motif

**MANGAASI
CULTURE**
c.600 BC–AD 1200

LAPITA CULTURE IN MELANESIA AND WESTERN POLYNESIA
c.2000–100 BC

Relief showing
Assyrian king
killing a lion

Temple of Karnak:
Hypostyle Hall,
c.1290 BC

ASSYRIAN EMPIRE
883–612 BC

**BABYLONIAN
EMPIRE**
612–539 BC

EGYPT: NEW KINGDOM
c.1550–1070 BC

HITTITE EMPIRE
c.1400–1200 BC

PHOENICIAN TRADE EXPANDS IN MEDITERRANEAN
c.900–600 BC

Phoenician ship

ETRUSCAN CIVILIZATION
c.800–300 BC

MYCENAEAN CIVILIZATION
c.1600–1100 BC

EARLY GREEK CITY STATES
c.750–500 BC

Gold death
mask

CELTIC HALLSTATT CULTURE
c.800–500 BC

The
Buddha
c.560–480 BC

Harness
fitting

SHANG DYNASTY
c.1600–1027 BC

**WESTERN
ZHOU PERIOD**
1027–770 BC

ZHOU "SPRING AND AUTUMN" PERIOD
c.770–481 BC

Bronze
ritual
vessel

| 1400 BC | 1200 BC | 1100 BC | 1000 BC | 900 BC | 800 BC | 700 BC | 600 BC | 500 BC |

Timelines 2

| | 500 BC | 400 BC | 300 BC | 200 BC | 100 BC | AD 1 | 100 | | 300 | 400 |

AMERICAS

OLMEC CULTURE
c.1200–400 BC

Warrior-shaped pot

MOCHE CULTURE
c.200 BC–AD 600

CHAVÍN CULTURE
c.850–200 BC

NAZCA CULTURE
c.350 BC–AD 600

AUSTRALASIA AND OCEANIA

LAPITA CULTURE IN MELANESIA AND WESTERN POLYNESIA
c.2000–100 BC

COLONIZATION OF HAWAII AND EASTER ISLAND
c.100–400

Sailing canoe

MIDDLE EAST AND AFRICA

PERSIAN ACHAEMENID EMPIRE
c.550–331 BC

PERSIA: PARTHIAN DYNASTY
c.247 BC–AD 226

PERSIA: SASSANIAN DYNASTY
c.226–651

Coin showing Sassanian king

Gold armlet from Oxus Treasure

Cameo of Emperor Augustus

Jesus Christ
c.4 BC–AD 29

EUROPE

ROMAN REPUBLIC
509–27 BC

ROMAN EMPIRE
27 BC–AD 476

ETRUSCAN CIVILIZATION
c.800–300 BC

Porta Nigra, Germany, c.180

CLASSICAL GREECE
c.500–330 BC

Celtic shield

CELTIC LA TÈNE CULTURE
c.500 BC–AD 50

INDIA AND THE FAR EAST

MAURYAN EMPIRE
c.320–185 BC

SATAVAHANA DYNASTY
c.200 BC–AD 250

GUPTA EMPIRE
c.320–500

HAN DYNASTY
206 BC–AD 220

Lion-headed capital

KOFUN PERIOD
c.300–600

Haniwa figure of a warrior

| | 400 BC | 300 BC | 200 BC | 100 BC | AD 1 | 100 | | 400 |

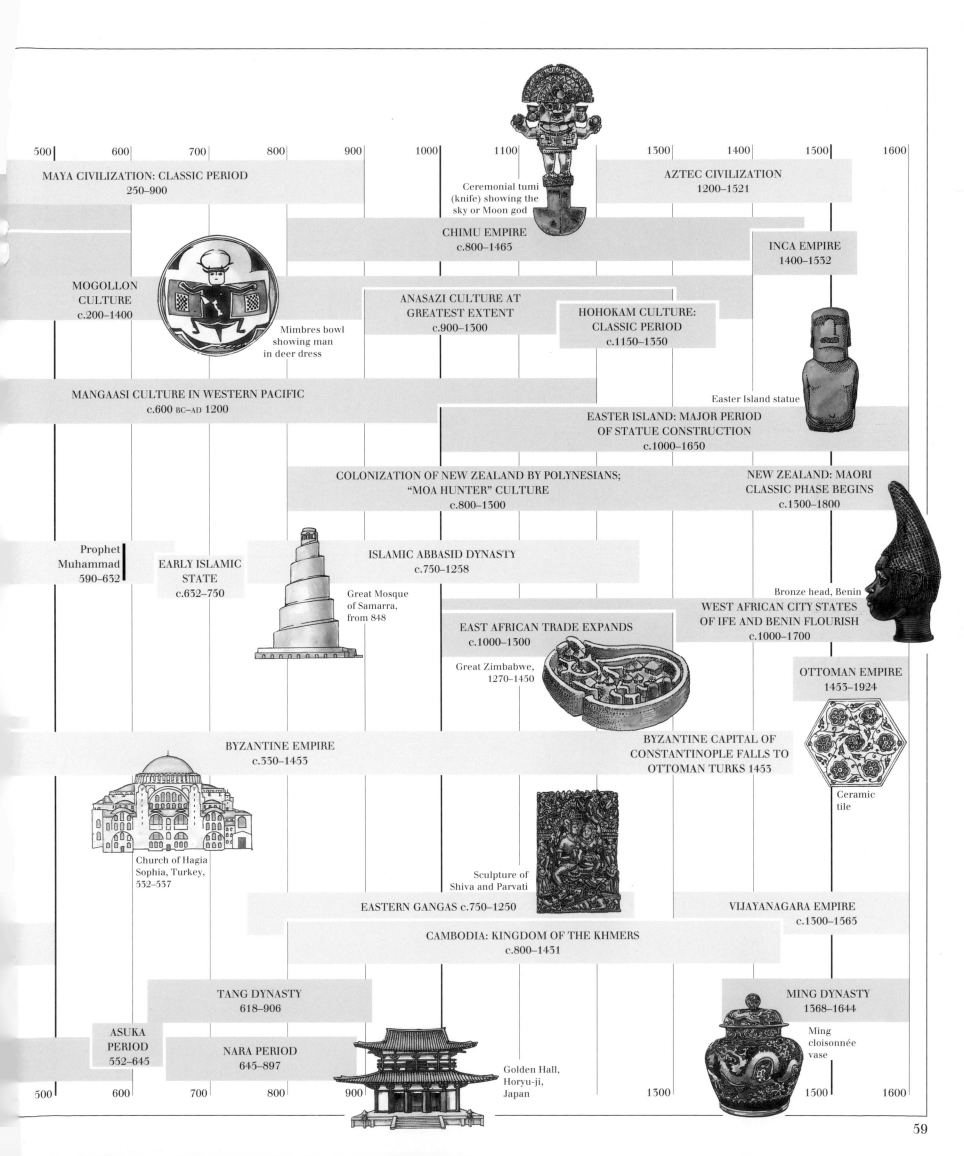

500　600　700　800　900　1000　1100　1300　1400　1500　1600

MAYA CIVILIZATION: CLASSIC PERIOD
250–900

Ceremonial tumi
(knife) showing the
sky or Moon god

AZTEC CIVILIZATION
1200–1521

CHIMU EMPIRE
c.800–1465

INCA EMPIRE
1400–1532

**MOGOLLON
CULTURE**
c.200–1400

**ANASAZI CULTURE AT
GREATEST EXTENT**
c.900–1300

**HOHOKAM CULTURE:
CLASSIC PERIOD**
c.1150–1350

Mimbres bowl
showing man
in deer dress

MANGAASI CULTURE IN WESTERN PACIFIC
c.600 BC–AD 1200

Easter Island statue

**EASTER ISLAND: MAJOR PERIOD
OF STATUE CONSTRUCTION**
c.1000–1650

**COLONIZATION OF NEW ZEALAND BY POLYNESIANS;
"MOA HUNTER" CULTURE**
c.800–1300

**NEW ZEALAND: MAORI
CLASSIC PHASE BEGINS**
c.1300–1800

Prophet
Muhammad
590–632

**EARLY ISLAMIC
STATE**
c.632–750

ISLAMIC ABBASID DYNASTY
c.750–1258

Great Mosque
of Samarra,
from 848

Bronze head, Benin

**WEST AFRICAN CITY STATES
OF IFE AND BENIN FLOURISH**
c.1000–1700

EAST AFRICAN TRADE EXPANDS
c.1000–1300

Great Zimbabwe,
1270–1450

OTTOMAN EMPIRE
1453–1924

BYZANTINE EMPIRE
c.330–1453

**BYZANTINE CAPITAL OF
CONSTANTINOPLE FALLS TO
OTTOMAN TURKS 1453**

Ceramic
tile

Church of Hagia
Sophia, Turkey,
532–537

Sculpture of
Shiva and Parvati

EASTERN GANGAS c.750–1250

VIJAYANAGARA EMPIRE
c.1300–1565

CAMBODIA: KINGDOM OF THE KHMERS
c.800–1431

TANG DYNASTY
618–906

MING DYNASTY
1368–1644

Ming
cloisonné
vase

**ASUKA
PERIOD**
552–645

NARA PERIOD
645–897

Golden Hall,
Horyu-ji,
Japan

500　600　700　800　900　1300　1500　1600

Index

Acknowledgments

Dorling Kindersley would like to thank:
The Trustees and the staff of the Departments of the British Museum, London, in particular James Putnam, Anne Farrer, Herma Chang, and Jim Hamill; The National Trust; Frances Wood of the British Library, London

Picture credits:
(t=top, b=bottom, c=centre, l=left, r=right)
All photography from the British Museum, London except for:
Archiv fur Kunst front cover, 24cr (Herakleion Museum, Crete); 25t (Erich Lessing, National Archeological Museum, Athens); front cover, 18tr (Erich Lessing, Louvre Museum, Paris).
Ashmolean Museum, Oxford front cover; 6tl; 20tl; 25bl.
Collection Tony Berlant, Santa Monica, CA 5cr; 45cr.
Dr. J. Biel, Landesdemkmalant Baden-Württemberg, Stuttgart 22cl; 22b.
Bildarchiv Preussischer Kulturbesitz 19 (Klaus Goken, Berlin State Museum).
Bridgeman Art Library 21b (Louvre Museum, Paris).
British Library Board, London 53bl.
Cambridge University Museum of Archaeology

and Anthropology 40tr; 42tl; 43tr.
Andy Crawford 34tl.
Darmstadt Museum 34-35b; 35t.
C.M. Dixon 24br (Herakleion Museum, Crete).
Werner Forman Archive 42tr (Museum für Völkerkunde, Berlin); 44tl (Arizona State Museum); 45tr (Maxwell Museum of Anthropology, Albuquerque).
James Harpur 26cl.
Michael Holford 42bl; 42br; 52bl (Cernuschi Museum, Paris).
Museums of Scotland 32tl; 37tcl; 54cc.
INAH, Mexican Museum Authority (Michel Zabé) 38bl; 38bc; 38br; 40tl; 41tr; 41br; 42br.
Image Bank (Charles C. Place) 45tl.
Justin Kerr, New York front cover; 2–3bc; 38tr; 39.
The National Trust 5br; 48bl.
Ruth Midgley 24tl.
Peabody Museum, Harvard University (Hillel Burger) 44tcr; 44tr; 45br.
Royal Photographic Society (Francis Frith) 11cl.
Sir John Soanes Museum, London 26b.
Scala, Florence 24bl (Herakleion Museum, Crete); 28tl (National Museum of Athens); 32br (Vatican); 33; 36br (Uffizi).
The Science Museum, London 34bl.

Collection of the Tokyo National Museum 54bl; 54bc; 54r.
University of Tennessee 10-11b.

Additional photography:
Alan Hills, Ivor Kerslake, David Gower, Nick Nicholls, Peter Hayman, Kevin Lovelock, Christi Graham (The British Museum); Michel Zabé; Geoff Brightling; Karl Shone

Additional editorial assistance:
David Harding

Additional artwork:
Russell Barnett 34

Index:
Kay Wright

Picture Research:
Valya Alexander; Caroline Brooke